Host Family
Survival Kit

With the compliments of

ERDT / **SHARE!**

Educational Resource Development Trust
SHARE! High School Exchange Program

1-800-321-3738

Host Family Survival Kit

A Guide for American Host Families

Second Edition

Nancy King and Ken Huff

INTERCULTURAL PRESS, INC.

First published by Intercultural Press. For information contact:

Intercultural Press, Inc.
PO Box 700
Yarmouth, Maine 04096 USA
207-846-5168
Fax: 207-846-5181
www.interculturalpress.com

Nicholas Brealey Publishing
3-5 Spafield St.
London, EC1R 4QB,UK
44-207-239-0360
Fax: 44-207-239-0370
www.nbrealey-books.com

Book design and production: Patty J. Topel
Cover illustration: Tom Brown

Printed in the United States of America

08 07 06 05 04   6 7 8 9

Library of Congress Cataloging-in-Publication Data
King, Nancy.

King, Nancy.
   Host family survival kit: a guide for American host families/ Nancy King and Ken Huff.—2nd ed.
     p. cm.
   ISBN 1-877864-37-4
   1. Student exchange programs—United States. 2. Host families of foreign students—United States. I. Huff, Ken.
II. Title.
LB1696.K56   1997
370.116—dc21   97-30489
                                         CIP

Table of Contents

Foreword

Hosting a foreign exchange student for a school year is potentially one of the most rewarding experiences that any family can have, if they are prepared to do the work that is required to grow as individuals and as a family.

My wife, Lynn, and I have hosted four young women to date. This makes us more experienced than some and far less experienced than others. We have also worked with other students and families as local volunteers for one of the major exchange organizations. Each of the students that we have hosted has been from a different country (Italy, Finland, Germany, and Norway). Each has had a major impact on our lives during the time that she was with us. That impact continues because of the memories they gave us, the continued correspondence, and the occasional visits—in both directions.

We have come to realize that exchange students are very special people, extraordinary in many ways. They are courageous enough and curious enough to venture away from their homes, families, and cultures to embrace the unfamiliar by spending a year with people they don't yet know in a place filled with new discoveries.

Host families must be equally courageous and inquisitive if they are to maximize the rewards. When you agree to host a student, you are accepting a young person from another culture into the privacy of your home. When you make the initial decision, you will know relatively little about this new person and probably little about his or her culture. During your time together, you will face challenges and the entire family will grow.

It has certainly happened in our family. Lynn and I have had to learn to accept views of everyday life and of the world which differ from those which we held so firmly before. We have had to examine our own culture, our own language, and many of our beliefs. As we have looked inward, we have become more accepting of our own American culture and also more critical.

It's nothing if not amazing. That's how we would describe all the learning that takes place for both the family and student during their time together. When else have we been asked to explain subtleties of language, such as precisely when to use the word *many* and when to use the word *much*? Such questions often make us stop in our tracks and really think.

We have also had to think about why we do things a certain way either as a family or as a nation. An answer like "just because" is simply not enough. We have been forced to examine our family life, culture, and national values. Change is often the inevitable result of such self-examination. And it is always change for the better.

Lynn and I did not discover *Host Family Survival Kit* until we were halfway through our second hosting experience. What a shame, for this book is full of insights and practical advice which would have made hosting so much easier for us. I can think of no better way for you and your entire family to prepare than for every member over the age of twelve to read this book!

You probably realize that no two exchange students are the same, and no two host families either. Thus, every exchange experience is unique. The timing of the various "stages" which are described in this book will be different for each family and student, and some of the stages may not even occur or may pass with hardly any notice. Yet you will find the generalizations useful in giving you a realistic set of expectations.

Should you expect there to be some problems along the way? There almost certainly will be problems to some degree or other, for that is the nature of human interaction. It simply isn't natural for people to get along in perfect harmony all the time. We think that the important thing is to know how to recognize any friction that might occur and then to know how to address it. A big plus of this book is that it will give you some tools to do both.

To our way of thinking, there are at least three key ingredients for a successful exchange. As we mentioned earlier, the willingness to grow and change is fundamental. The ability to recognize cultural differences as neither good nor bad, just different, is another. The patience to really listen, to really hear, to really see, and to really think is also vital. As you might well imagine, all of this requires a relatively stable family, with sufficient maturity to be able to do the work that is necessary for success.

It probably goes without saying that a severely dysfunctional family should not consider hosting. By doing so, they will only exacerbate the dysfunction. Nor should a family accept an exchange student for their own advantage. An exchange student will not heal a troubled marriage, will not provide a free babysitter or a best friend for a family's own kids, and will not cause an alcoholic to drink less. Indeed, with the addition of an exchange student, the marriage may disintegrate faster; the student will likely feel resentment for being treated as a servant; your own children may become lonelier, bitter, or jealous; and the alcoholic may well drink more.

Our first student came to us as what's called a "re-placement." She arrived in early October after the mother and father in her first host family decided to divorce. My wife and I had talked about hosting earlier, and when the local representative asked us to take Mirella into our home and hearts, we said yes. It was an experience that changed our lives.

We can tell you that taking a student at the last minute may well lead to a wonderful relationship, but we have come to know the importance of carefully "shopping" for an exchange student in order to greatly increase the odds of success. We look at the summary materials and the full applications, gleaning as much information about each candidate as we can before making a final decision. Then comes the fun of writing that first letter to the student, making the first phone call, getting to know more about her, and letting her learn more about us. Within a couple of months the student has a pretty good idea of who we are, how we live, and what we will be expecting. Conversely, we have a good idea of who she is also. We have time to adjust to each other before we are together, face to face.

We have come to understand that we have much to learn from other cultures and much to share as well. Our lives have been greatly enriched by the four young women we have hosted. Each is different; each has won our hearts. We strongly believe that each has the ability, in her own way, to make a significant difference in the world during her lifetime. They are remarkable young women whom we otherwise would never have known. We are very rich indeed.

We strongly suggest that you do all that you can to prepare yourself for hosting. Read this book, then read it again. Use it as a starting point and a reference. Just remember, there is no "cookbook formula" which can guarantee a hosting success; there is no exact recipe. You may well need to add more of one ingredient or less of another. We urge you, however, to take the many useful concepts and tools offered in *Host Family Survival Kit* and create a fabulous feast for yourself and the students you host. Armed with the knowledge contained in this book, you can create an experience that has the power to change lives—yours and your student's.

Dr. Walter Kendall and his wife, Lynn, live in Colorado. He is president of a marketing research company, and she is vice president of an energy consulting firm.

Acknowledgments

Our thanks are extended to the countless families, students, colleagues, and friends whose insights and experiences appear throughout this book.

Part I

An Overview of the Hosting Experience

—1—

Baseball, Apple Pie, and Pickled Fish in Bottles

What on earth could pickled fish possibly have in common with baseball and apple pie? And what does the combination have to do with hosting a foreign exchange student?

"Pickled fish in bottles" is our way of describing the "foreignness" of foreigners. Beyond the border of the United States, fish is a delicacy that is savored raw (Japan), bottled in a spicy brine (Scandinavia), or marinated with salted lime and lemon juice (South America). But most people in the United States like fish only when it is thoroughly cooked—better yet when it is filleted, breaded, and deep fried.

You know the stage has been set for the melding of two very different cultures when a baseball-loving American* family serves its foreign exchange student a juicy, sweet slice of apple pie. The well-meaning student reciprocates by opening up a bottle and offering in return a prized treat of tangy pickled fish with head and eyes fully intact. Being unaccustomed to rich desserts, the student nibbles at the pie while the family

---

* With the full knowledge that the Americas include North, Central, and South America, we are using the word *American* in this book to refer specifically to the people living in the United States. This usage was chosen because of its vernacular popularity, not because of a lack of appreciation for the many cultures and nationalities that are equally American.

picks courteously at the fish. The result: stomachs from both cultures churn, but the mix of surprise and curiosity generated by this encounter opens the way for a cross-cultural experience of exciting proportions—one with the potential of being at once hilarious, tender, bewildering, and enriching.

The intertwining of differences and the development of international friendships are what cross-cultural encounters are all about. It is the intent of this book to explore with you the nature of such encounters and to provide guidance—a survival kit—for a successful experience. As we spend the next 200 or so pages together, we hope to prepare your spirit—if not your digestive tract—for "pickled fish in bottles" and a thousand other curiosities, surprises, and unexpected treats that occur when cultures come together.

How did all this get started? Although hundreds of international teenage exchange programs exist today, the concept got its start in the aftermath of World War II. At that time, by encouraging NATO-alliance youth to take up residence in the United States and by exporting American teenagers to live with European families, the United States hoped to both make friends abroad and increase understanding.

As originally conceived, European teenagers would live with an American family in the United States for a year and, typically, attend high school. The American family would agree to provide room, board, and a generous slice of American life. In return, the teenager would impart knowledge about his or her country, thereby enriching the family with the customs and traditions of distant lands. A program fee would cover airfare, orientation, support services, medical backup, and in some cases language training.

While this remains the most common exchange pattern, over the years the original mission—to widen circles of friendship between Americans and Europeans—has been expanded. Foreign teenagers from more than 120 countries around the globe are arriving in the United States each year. And almost an equal number of countries host American youth. Of the 400-plus sponsoring programs, many stress the study abroad aspect, requiring solid academic credentials and language proficiency. Many programs place primary importance on the personal growth that occurs with the family living experience. Their literature reminds the reader that if it's cultural learning you are seeking, the overseas family is the world's greatest classroom. Other programs appeal to the adolescent's love of high adventure and quest for identity by enticing the student with the challenge, "Find yourself in another world."

In addition to the standard type of exchange, there are some newer, hybrid varieties: a domestic exchange student program within the United States; arrangements for placing teenagers in alternative group-living situations such as with archeological projects or on farm collectives; a student ambassador program; short-term summer homestays which may highlight language training, computer literacy, visits to historical sites, or participation in art institutes. High on the adventure scale, one summer program in New Zealand includes a six-week safari. And high on the competition scale, the popular "Sports for Understanding" program meshes athletic training with an international experience. Equally important, youth from Russia, Romania, Uzbekistan, and other states and satellites of the former Soviet Union are now spending a year in the United States under the auspices of government partner programs designed to open lines of communication.

As a result, hundreds of thousands of young people have participated in overseas homestay programs, and today the globe is virtually encircled by exchange organizations which provide a smorgasbord of cross-cultural options. Young people are placed in small towns, sleepy hamlets, and bustling metropolitan centers; they take up residence in tongue-twister cities like Reykjavik, Iceland, or exotic Jakarta, Indonesia. Students travel to both northern and southern hemispheres, live with families of Muslim, Shinto, Christian, Jewish, Buddhist, or other religious persuasion—or of no religious persuasion—and are exposed to the political creeds of both developing and highly industrialized nations.

During the summer months when hundreds of students arrive and depart en masse, international airports become friendly mob scenes. And, on a year-round basis, e-mail and faxes zipping across continents announce to natural parents: *"Congratulations! Host family found for your daughter"* or *"Please write to horribly homesick son"* or *"Student broke! Send money soonest."*

Indeed, hosting now touches the lives of thousands of Americans and in some cases two or more generations. With the arrival of the twenty-first century, it's not uncommon to find third-generation exchange students living with hosts who are themselves former exchangees. Many American families regularly receive letters and mementos from a number of former exchange students who at one time or another shared a year with them. Of the thousands of students who have participated in homestay experiences, some have gone on to become world leaders, mayors and governors, international policymakers, and corporate executives for multinational businesses. Student exchange has grown dramatically, creating a gigantic network of teenagers, host and natural families, overseas and domestic community volunteers, professionals, and dignitaries.

Again and again host families return to the sponsoring organizations, wanting once more to bring a young person from another land into their homes and hearts. As they have crossed cultures to build new friendships and an extended international family, their lives have become more interesting, their tolerance has grown, and their sensitivities have expanded. Hosting has exposed them to hundreds of opportunities to sample "pickled fish in bottles" and other equally unexpected yet savory treats.

All this brings us back to where we started: the American host family whose student thanked them with a bottle of her country's finest pickled herring. Although they were squeamish about tasting it, they discovered to their amazement that they liked pickled herring...at least somewhat. Years later, we can imagine them as they find themselves joking about "those pickled fish in bottles" while shopping for this delicacy at a neighborhood market. They may chuckle at the memory of their hesitant first bite, for now it is something they enjoy at their Sunday brunch buffet: pickled herring with sour cream on a plate with egg salad, bagel, lox, kugel, and a slice of sweet challah.

Like these acquired tastes, we hope you find that hosting grows on you.

—2—

What Exactly Is an Exchange Student?

Is there a particular role that an exchange student is expected to assume? Is he or she similar to a new family member? A weekend houseguest? A neighborhood friend? A cleaning woman? Or what?

People who live together as a family develop a bond of shared experiences, hold common expectations, and act more casually than they would at work or in other public places. At home, family members know they can let their hair down and relax. It matters little if someone yawns in the middle of a conversation or neglects to stifle a burp. Likewise, addressing each other by affectionate nicknames (such as Sis or Motormouth) or diminutives (Katherine becomes "K.T.") is encouraged.

In some households, family members can dash about in a modified version of their birthday suit and no one seems to mind. They also know not to bring up certain subjects that arouse unpleasant memories. And no one gets seriously upset when children occasionally treat each other shabbily or parents complain about neglected household chores.

But when an old college classmate or a favorite aunt visits for the weekend, the situation becomes very different. The family brings out the guest towels and the good silver. Everyone puts on his or her best manners (that means burps are temporarily taboo), appears properly attired, and showers the guest with attention, food, and heartwarming entertainment. In other words, the houseguest is to be treated royally and, in a certain sense, the family is on trial. Indeed, it is the family's duty, if not privilege, to serve.

While entertaining the weekend guest, formalities are both bearable and functional. The host makes sure that polite euphemisms are used with guests and is careful not to cause discomfort or embarrassment. Unpleasant experiences are referred to cautiously and matters of health and hygiene are inquired about ever so gently by stating rhetorically, "Please let us know if you need anything."

Neighborhood pals are another matter. When the children's friends come to visit—no matter what the purpose— it is the *visitors* who are on trial, who must prove themselves worthy of house privileges. Thus, knowing they must be on their best behavior, neighborhood friends tend to be polite, courteous, and are rarely spoilsports.

Not only are neighborhood friends expected to learn and abide by the family rules, they are also expected to know not to stay for dinner unless repeatedly invited, that certain areas of the house are off-limits, and that teasing younger family members is forbidden. Friends who overstep these invisible boundaries are labeled ill-mannered, and if their behavior doesn't improve, they are admonished: you're not welcome here anymore!

If the family has a cleaning woman, she is treated like neither a family member, an honored guest, nor a neighborhood friend. Unlike the houseguest and neighbor, who must limit their comings and goings to public areas, she is free to move about and even required to inspect every nook and cranny. It seems clear to everyone what the arrangement is: the housekeeper offers a cleaning service; the family offers payment—a basic trade-off.

When you think about it, the role of the housekeeper or cleaning woman is an intriguing paradox: she is both intimately involved with the family and at the same time extremely detached. In many ways she may know more about you and your family's business than your closest friend. Yet families feign ignorance of the cleaning woman's presence or knowing eyes. What she sees and hears or thinks seems to matter naught, because everyone in the household assumes it is the cleaning woman's job to scrub, not scrutinize. Secondly, her status is such that family members would courteously disregard her opinions even if she were to offer any (live-in help and nannies are sometimes exceptions to this rule). And, perhaps most important, the cleaning woman has learned that her job is to see but to pretend that she doesn't.

As you may gather, our ways of behaving at home vary greatly depending on whom we are with. We have distinct although familiar ways of relating to family, to houseguests, to visiting neighbor friends, and to hired help. *But what we don't have are familiar and traditional ways of relating to someone who comes from a foreign country for an extended stay in our home.*

Too often, host families try to place their new exchange student in one of the familiar roles that have just been described. Why? Because it is human nature to apply what we already know and are comfortable with to new situations. There is nothing wrong with this, of course, except for the fact that the exchange student–host family relationship does not fit into a familiar category. Trying to pretend that it does is like attempting to mold an extraordinary gem with an unusual shape into a traditional piece of jewelry. There is never a truly satisfying fit. And in the process, a marvelous opportunity to experience something entirely new is missed.

Let's look at why this is so.

Family Member Role

If exchange students could be brought home and somehow plugged in like a new toaster, then instantaneously and definitively they would become an integral part of a host family. But relationships and loyalties don't happen that easily. Family bonds are created from participation in a common family culture of interwoven routines, years of shared experiences, and a unique combination of intimacy, devotion, growth, conflict, and loyalty.

So when exchange students are encouraged prematurely to think of their hosts as family and are pressured to call their host parents "Mom" and "Dad,"* conflicts of allegiance can develop. The student may feel guilty for betraying his or her natural family by adopting a competing one or may worry that the hosts will feel rejected if they are not embraced in this honored way.

Of course, there are situations (especially after spending several months with a host family) when exchange students become so comfortable that they say they, in fact, feel like a family member. But achieving this kind of closeness takes time, and at first most students do not feel like a family member even if assured that they are. For example, when the family visits close relatives and reminisces with them, the student is likely to feel awkward. When holidays and birthdays are celebrated, the student may, at best, feel only partly involved. And, although students may eagerly attend services to learn about U.S. religious practices, they are nonetheless likely to feel like outsiders.

Houseguest Role

For a host family to become excited about having a foreigner live in its home is pretty normal. Also, many families fret about whether they will do what is "right" to help the student feel comfortable during the first hours and days. And all families seem to work hard at extending an enthusiastic welcome. For all of these reasons—excitement, doubt, concern—host families frequently begin treating their exchange students as houseguests. Wanting to please and entertain, they may unwittingly hoist the students up on a pedestal. Such students find it difficult to assume their role as human beings who have the task of adjusting to a new living environment.

---

* Frequently, host parents will invite their student to address them as "Mom" and "Dad." We see no problem with this as long as the student is comfortable with the arrangement and as long as it is understood that the host family is not assuming a role that will preempt or rival the role of the student's natural parents. For more details, please refer to the section in chapter 10 entitled, "Decisions about Names."

And what about the host family? The situation boils down to this: realistically, how long can someone go without yawning or burping at the wrong time? Is it reasonable to assume that a host family can entertain, cater to, sacrifice for, play up to, and pamper an exchange student day after day for six weeks, six months, or a full year? Our hunch is that by trying, nerves will soon get frazzled and resentments begin to fester.

Imagine what might happen if you began treating the exchange student in your home like a houseguest who is visiting for a three-day weekend. You obviously would not broach the subject of body functions to inquire whether or not the person is constipated from traveling. After all, you assume that a guest will know how to discreetly handle the situation.

You would courteously show houseguests where the clean towels are kept, but you wouldn't need to demonstrate how to use the shower or toilet. The guest would have the following routine down pat: the shower curtain belongs on the inside of the tub, and the plumbing works well enough so that it is not necessary—as is customary in some parts of the world—to throw used toilet paper in the trash can. Moreover, while guests may wish to hand-wash some items, most would not be staying so long that they would need to learn where to put dirty underwear or when to change the bed linens. You also would not need to tell houseguests where to buy tampons or how to dispose of them without clogging the drainpipes or where to obtain birth control products.[†]

And what about finances? You can bet that a houseguest won't arrive with a rubber-banded wad of hundred-dollar bills or a million Italian lira stuffed in a suitcase. You assume that the guest has traveler's checks and can handle money matters for the duration of the brief vacation. After all, a houseguest can typically handle U.S. currency, and there would

---

[†] Of course, exchange students are not necessarily sexually active, and we are by no means suggesting that exchange students should be using birth control. But as a host parent, it is important for you to let your student know that you are available to discuss such matters if the need arises.

be no logical reason to suggest that a checking account be opened.

But with the arrival of an exchange student, many of these exquisitely sensitive, painfully intimate matters—matters which you rarely discuss with a houseguest—may need addressing. On a few occasions in the past when these issues have been overlooked, families have found themselves dealing with dreadfully embarrassing problems.

Neighborhood Friend Role

Problems can also develop when an exchange student is viewed as a visiting neighborhood friend. Just as your family would be miserable trying to be gracious hosts for months on end, so it is nerve-racking for an exchange student who tries to be the forever obedient and polite visitor, hyperalert day and night in order to avoid giving offense.

Also, if the family mistakenly believes that the student is here primarily to have a good time, how can the daily boring routines be camouflaged, or the serious moments jazzed up to make every second a roller coaster of thrills and excitement? Moreover, where can you send an exchange student who gets sick or mouthy, since the student's home is not down the street or around the corner? Unlike the neighborhood teenager who visits for a few brief hours and then is gone, the exchange student stays on in your household.

Hired Help Role

Few host families accept an exchange student with the obvious intent of acquiring live-in help—such as a babysitter, cleaning woman, or handyman. Still, the expectations of some families are such that the student gets the impression that the relationship is purely one of exchanged services. This is the unspoken contract: the family agrees to provide room and board, and the student repays in gratitude by never complaining and doing whatever job is assigned. When reduced to traded services grounded in obligations, a relationship which initially brimmed with spontaneity and generosity can wither into something dry and bitter.

There's a second reason why exchange students don't make good housekeepers: they don't play by the rules for hired help. With an exchange student rummaging around and ultimately exploring every bottle and basket in a restless need to understand the new environment, the family has on its hands a "cleaning woman" or a "handyman" with the curiosity of Sherlock Holmes! Students see, they acknowledge what they see, and they put clues together to reach conclusions. Being on a par with the family, what the student sees and how she or he reacts may have a powerful effect. As one host parent expressed it, "At times, you feel yourself observed, painfully exposed, and probably judged."

To Sum Up

You may feel uneasy at the prospect of being scrutinized in the privacy of your home, having your personal comfort jostled for more than a few days, or talking about sensitive topics with the stranger who is your exchange student. If so, it is hardly surprising. It might reassure you to know that few experienced host families would describe the experience as a year of nothing but comfortable conversations. They say it is hard work, with a yield of ample rewards.

To make the experience rewarding for you personally, you may need to know more about the hosting relationship. In this chapter, we've suggested how not to relate. In the next couple of chapters, we suggest some ways that may prove helpful.

—3—

Host Parenting:
It's Something Grand

Just as we don't have a quick and ready idea of what an exchange student is, we also don't have familiar categories for host parents. Obviously, they aren't the same as birth parents. Nor is hosting a teenager anything like adopting a newborn. At first glance, one might liken them to parents who adopt a child of adolescent age, since such parents are taking over for previous caregivers who have already shaped the adoptee's personality and behavior. But unlike teenage adoptees, foreign exchange students will not always be aware of the way one is supposed to behave in the United States.

As we scan the horizon in search of a definition for a host parent, there's just not much we can point our finger at and say, "There's what we mean. That's what a host parent is." We can, however, give you some ideas about what a host parent is not. A host parent is not responsible for molding the exchange student's personality; the natural parents took care of that long ago. Nor is it the host parents' job to make sure the exchange student is growing up to become a responsible adult. That also is the natural parents' role, and besides, what we define as responsible behavior in the United States isn't necessarily the same as in the student's home country. Why would you try to turn an exchange student into a "good" American when that might have the effect of making him a "bad" Asian?

Certainly the host parent does act as a caregiver, seeing to it that the exchange student is properly housed, fed, and protected from harm. And hosts have a very important teaching role. But a host parent is more than a caregiver and teacher, although still less than a true parent. A host parent seems to be one step removed from the direct responsibilities of a natural parent. And if you give it some thought, you may realize that there already is a model for such a role: your grandparents.

Remember what it was like when you visited your grandparents' home? You probably loved it. You were smothered with affection, and it was both fascinating and strange—like being in a different world, another culture. There were many things they said and did that seemed old-fashioned. You weren't entirely comfortable with their slower-paced lifestyle, and they talked of an era you could hardly imagine: a time when nobody locked their doors at night, and when they could buy a bag of candy for a few pieces of change.

Of course, lots of grandparents today are living in Sunbelt retirement communities and playing daily rounds of golf, but when it comes to their style of relating to the grandchildren, an effective grandparent still behaves much the same. Grandparents have been through the parental experience. They have taught their own children how to behave, disciplined them when necessary, and watched over their schooling with an exacting eye. They have worried about being a failure and about their children's future.

As grandparents, they can just forget most of the parental worries and concerns. They do teach their grandchildren things and are concerned about their adjustment and happiness, but for the most part they can now just plain get a lot of enjoyment from their grandchildren—as you can from your exchange student.

Another characteristic of effective grandparents is this: they realize that the world they grew up in isn't the same as the world their grandchildren have to cope with in the present. You might say that, for them, the past is like one culture and the present is another. So wise grandparents see the folly in trying to apply certain aspects of their wisdom to future generations. After all, what good does it do to admonish a granddaughter to "pinch your pennies 'til they cry" while she's busily beta testing new shareware on her pricey $2,000 computer?

When the modern teenage culture mystifies a grandparent, sensitivity is what is called for. And sensitive is what you, as a host parent, need to be by accepting that it is best to be more tolerant when chunks of what you know about your own culture don't necessarily apply to someone else's.

We can sum up two important functions of effective grandparents as follows:

1. They don't feel personally responsible for misbehavior.[1]

2. They are cautious about imposing their own experience and wisdom (culture), since this may not be particularly appropriate.

So while we can't say exactly what a host parent is, we can get you started in the right direction: hosting an exchange student requires a dash of the parenting skills you have already used with your own children blended with a large helping of the calmer, more reflective, and less directive approach of a grandparent.

In sum, hosting an exchange student means relating to a visitor in a new way, using a modified, blended style of teaching, parenting, and grandparenting. The realization that there is no prepackaged "set of rules" about how to proceed can be a bit disconcerting. However, people who have been hosting for a number of years have thoughtfully observed and described some of the characteristics of host family–exchange student relationships. Their observations are offered in the following chapters, along with suggestions intended to provide guidance and encouragement for an enriching, enjoyable, and successful hosting experience.

Endnotes

[1] Robert A. Aldrich and Glenn Austin, *Grandparenting for the 90s* (Escondido, CA: Robert Erdmann, 1991), 51.

—4—

What Is Hosting All About?

Seasoned host families reflect on their experience as follows:
- The student is here to learn about American family life from an insider's point of view, but although an inside learner, the student remains essentially an outsider to long-standing family ties, the family's shared history, and the special sense of loyalty felt exclusively by family members.
- As a learner and friend, the exchange student participates in the family's day-to-day activities. Through discussions, the student learns about the family's values, beliefs, outlook, and historical roots. Over time, and with continued involvement, the student usually develops a strong friendship with family members, a relationship of deep caring and mutual regard, and may eventually be regarded as an honorific family member.
- Through involvement with the family, the community, and high school, the student builds a foundation for understanding the culture of the United States.

Thus there appear to be two basic aspects to hosting a foreign student:
1. Sharing your lifestyle with a young person from another country, and
2. Providing a helping hand.

Lifestyle Sharing

You share your lifestyle by mapping out your particular style of living. Among other things, it means an awareness of and an ability to describe what you value in life and how those values are reflected in how you live—the things you do, the opinions you express, and the company you keep. Of course, much is learned by observation and through the course of daily living, but the more your lifestyle is discussed and clarified, the better.

You might start identifying your lifestyle by asking yourself what lifts your spirits the most. Is it puttering in your vegetable garden, attending hockey games, or working out at the neighborhood health club? If none of the above fit, perhaps you get a kick from surfing the Internet, pouring adrenaline into sixty-hour workweeks, or teaching a favorite Sunday school class.

Just as important are your family activities: the topics you discuss, the places you go, the things you do for fun. One mother and her daughter are regularly joined by a downstairs neighbor for "shake and quake" nights: they watch grade B horror movies and scare themselves silly. In another family, the children stage puppet shows for their parents or draw everyone (including visitors) into games featuring dolls, stuffed animals, and the dining room chairs. In still another family, everyone is a bathtub baritone or shower soprano during karaoke sing-alongs. You might not think these activities would hold any interest for an exchange student, but the moments families share with each other are precisely what build a sense of intimacy and belonging so crucial to lifestyle sharing.

It also is important to explain your family's beliefs and values: if you were polled, with what political persuasion, social causes, economic concerns, religious ideals, or national symbols would you identify? What ethnic traditions and ancestry make up your family heritage? Is yours a family of doers or talkers or thinkers? How would you rate the importance of such things as togetherness, achievement, open communication, or affection?

You will also want to describe whether your family is "traditional" or "nontraditional." Is yours a dual-income family? Or perhaps yours is a blended family, a single-parent family, an interracial family, or an extended family with grandparents or an aunt living in an attached apartment. These variations are a few of the many that have added new dimensions to the American landscape and warrant discussion.

Equally important, you will want to point out some things about your marital relationship and ideas about parenting. For example, is yours a hierarchical family or more egalitarian? Would you say your activities are child-centered, relationship-centered, or work-centered?

In short, lifestyle sharing means revealing what you and your family are all about. From the vast array of themes in our culture, which one best describes you? And, since families vary within themes, what makes your particular family unique?

One family who has hosted half-a-dozen times invites their student to become involved in their lifestyle but points out the reasons why they are not representative of the whole country:

> We're a jump-in-and-do, on-the-go family. We're involved with our church, the youth group, with clubs, and organizations,[1] and we do what we can for our friends and neighbors. But we let our exchange student know right off that Americans are not all the same. We say, "Our culture is made up of a dozen or more major ingredients. Our family is just one of the vegetables—not the whole beef stew."

How does a family go about describing its lifestyle and cultural traditions? First of all, it can take hour upon hour of discussion and explanation—combined with regular reference to a good bilingual dictionary in search of words that aren't part of the exchange student's vocabulary. As the couple quoted above explains,

> It's quite time-consuming to host a foreign student. You just don't explain things in two or three words. Sometimes we're up 'til three in the morning trying to sort things out.

As this kind of sharing develops, the process of accommoda-
tion to each other begins. It is probably realistic to expect
that the student will have to do most of the accommodating.
After all, the student is moving into the host family's lifestyle
and not vice versa. But some give-and-take by the host family
is critically necessary. The host family we have already quoted
continues:

> One year we had a French student who'd had her
> own apartment for two years. She'd grown accus-
> tomed to tossing dirty clothes in the closet, stack-
> ing dirty dishes in huge mounds, and living in the
> same T-shirt and jeans for weeks on end. We tried
> our darnedest to tolerate her ways, and we made
> some accommodations. But we had a clash of
> lifestyle until Nicole* felt she could comfortably con-
> form to our particular style of housekeeping.
>
> Another time we had a student who joined the
> local community theater group. We were all excited
> for her but were also stuck with a colossal schedul-
> ing dilemma. With my wife working evenings, our
> daughter taking dance lessons at six P.M. and our
> son going to Cub Scouts at seven, there was sud-
> denly no way I could work out at the Y and get
> Brigetta to rehearsals. Things had to be reshuffled,
> and when I found myself driving to the playhouse
> four nights a week, I began to feel like a regular
> there. But we all understood that this was impor-
> tant for Brigetta. We have absolutely no regrets
> about it but think the statement, "Having an ex-
> change student means just another mouth to feed,"
> should be forever stricken from the books. It ain't
> necessarily so.

Despite it all, this family notes that satisfying returns can come
from the hard work, aggravation, and long hours involved:

> All in all, it can be a lot of fun showing another
> person what your life is like. On Easter, we take

---

* The examples described in this book come from real-life situations.
Names, however, have been changed to insure anonymity.

our exchange student with us to the parish where we have our basket of food blessed. On Christmas Eve, we'll all be in the kitchen throwing together strange kinds of foods like *pierogi* [stuffed Polish dumplings], and our exchange student will be with us, elbow to elbow, and throwing questions our way.

Our parents come from the old school and preach, "Don't get involved with strangers. If you need help or want friends, that's what family is for." But we have a different sense of family; our friendships are not just with relatives. We enjoy teenagers, and for us, it's important to share our home with people from around the world. That kind of connectedness with the world at large matters a whole lot to us.

Clearly, lifestyle sharing with a foreign student can be rewarding, but it is not necessarily as easy as making social conversation at a cocktail party or having an interesting chat with a tourist. When it comes to relating to adolescents in general and foreign students in particular, host families can find themselves readily challenged, occasionally burdened, and frequently sought out for advice.

A Helping Hand in Wonderland

Many visitors to new countries and cultures experience a multitude of differences which can be confusing and sometimes seriously disorienting. In order to clarify how these differences affect people, let's take a look at an old story—*Alice's Adventures in Wonderland*—from a new perspective.

When Alice tumbled down the rabbit hole and spiraled dizzily into Wonderland, she crashed with a muddled thump in a bizarre and mystifying realm where she bumped and stumbled among strange and eerie creatures.

The "humans" Alice met seemed hardly humane. A grandiose duchess squeezed too close and muttered about "much of a muchness." "Take care of the sense, and the sounds will take care of themselves," Alice was chastised by people speaking a cacophony of platitudes, rhymes, and riddles. "She's nervous. Execute her!" someone thundered when Alice trembled with fear.

"You ought to be ashamed of asking such simple questions," a crowd shouted in her ear, leading Alice to blurt out in angry desperation, "There is no sense talking; these people are perfectly idiotic!" Lacking a book of rules to explain all the "frumious discomgollifustication" and feeling horribly confused, scolded, and forsaken, Alice began bowing to anyone and everything, bobbing like an errant yo-yo.

As Alice described it, "Everything became curiouser and curiouser." "What's happening to me?" she asked herself, muffling her dread. "How strange everything is today, and yesterday things went on as usual. It was so much pleasanter at home where one wasn't always growing larger and smaller, and being ordered about by mice and rabbits. I almost wish I hadn't gone down that rabbit hole—and yet—and yet—it's rather curious, you know, this sort of life. When I used to read fairy tales, I fancied this kind of thing never happened, and now, here I am in the middle of one."

If Alice were to have a friendly chat with a panel of modern-day social scientists, she might learn that when she left her familiar home and had feelings of alarm, confusion, and homesickness in Wonderland, she had experienced a case of culture shock.

Culture shock is a phrase which was popularized in 1958 by anthropologist Kalvero Oberg to describe the feelings of disorientation and anxiety that many people experience for a period of time while living in a foreign country. It results from the awareness that one's basic assumptions about life and one's familiar ways of behaving are no longer appropriate or functional.

When Alice entered Wonderland, she didn't know about culture shock, and she didn't think of Wonderland as a new and unfamiliar culture. But in a sense, that's what Wonderland was: a "foreign" culture where people related according to different expectations, where language was used differently to convey meaning, and where the rules for polite and reasonable behavior bore no resemblance to home. It was indeed unfortunate that Alice had no one to turn to, no one to help bridge her home culture and that of Wonderland.

Like Alice, many exchange students go through culture shock, as if they too had stumbled into Wonderland. They might feel awkwardly oversized or shrunken with insecurity. The home where they stay can appear upside down and backwards. Keys from the culture they have left behind don't always unlock the doors to comfortable relationships and understanding. Confused and disoriented, exchange students may perceive just about everything as utterly mystifying for a while. Thus, they often need help in the form of explanations, encouragement, and guidance. In short, they need a "cultural adviser."

A cultural adviser is a person who is both familiar with the new culture and willing to help explain the behavior of its inhabitants. As a host parent who is an expert on your family's lifestyle and as someone knowledgeable about American culture, you will probably be the one your student turns to for assistance.

At times, your help will be a matter of correcting the way words are pronounced or how language is used. Imagine your exchange student arriving home from his first day at school. He rushes in the door and begins to recount the day's events by saying, "My chemistry class in on the 'turd' floor." You may cringe at the thought of having to explain the difference between *turd* and *third*. But you soon realize that you really have no choice but to intervene; you know that the embarrassment will only intensify if you ignore it.

During your foreign student's stay, you will probably be called upon repeatedly to define such things as the meaning of unfamiliar words, to interpret slang, or to explain why describing one's sunny disposition by saying "I'm a gay person" might be misinterpreted. When your exchange student continually asks about such things, you may begin to bristle and be tempted to cut him or her short.†

---

† More information on language errors and the guidance you can give are provided in Appendix A, "Common Concerns."

Helping students with language is particularly important when they will be misunderstood or embarrassed because of their errors. Otherwise, it is probably best, at least in the beginning, not to place too much emphasis on correction. It's much more important to address the differences in behavior, attitudes, and values which emerge. The reason is this: differences in behavior, attitudes, and values have the potential for causing more serious problems than language errors ever could. Here's what we mean:

As with Alice in Wonderland, exchange students soon get an unsettling sense that things are getting "curiouser and curiouser." Old familiar ways of doing things no longer work. Finding this situation annoying, they often start to complain about everything, especially any obvious quirks and inconsistencies they have noticed. You might hear your student grumble and say:

- When you eat, why do you hold your fork so funny, with the prongs up instead of down?
- Why do you cover your mouth so politely when you yawn, but not when you hiccup?
- Why do you wash and rinse the dishes separately yet bathe and rinse yourself in the same bath water?

Repeated encounters with cultural differences might also begin to threaten your student's strongly held but largely out-of-awareness belief that there is one right way to do things. As a reaction, the student might mount a campaign of resistance—as was the case with a German student who struggled to hold tight to his belief in "one right way":

> Axel was a charming, polite boy who made friends immediately. That was good, but I was worried. I fretted that he was going to visit a girl's home, invite himself into her bedroom, and get thrown out by her father in two minutes flat.
>
> So every day for two weeks, I told Axel that American teenagers do not entertain friends in their bedrooms like they do in Europe. For two weeks he didn't believe me; he argued, questioned, and tried every possible way to explain away our custom.

His first reaction was to say, "If my English were better, I'm sure you'd agree with me. We're just not communicating." Next he discredited me and said, "You're crazy! You've got to be the only American who thinks like that." And he began bargaining with statements like, "Surely you're not talking about the daytime too, or with the door open." Then he just plain rejected what I said, "Well, that's stupid! The European way is better."

For all that time, what I was telling Axel just bounced off. Finally, after he had passed through all these mental steps, he accepted what I said as an accurate and sane message: In the U.S., no boys in girls' bedrooms, no girls in boys' bedrooms. That's the rule.

Sometimes exchange students find life in your home and community so different that they are immobilized by what for them is a Wonderland of "frumious discomgollifustication." Flávio, a thoughtful young Brazilian, felt so swept away by incomprehensible differences that he exclaimed:

In the U.S., water swirls down the drain clockwise instead of the counterclockwise Brazilian way, your coffee tastes like dishwater, the Southern Cross is missing from the night sky, the girls swear and talk about sex, and students are friends with their teachers. When I saw all this, I become lost in space. I thought, how can this be? I am really in a very different place!

As a cultural adviser, it will be your job to provide guidance and understanding about culture shock. To help with this seemingly daunting task, you will probably need to know something about invisible cultural baggage, deep culture, the stages of adjustment, and cross-cultural communication. These topics are presented next. Please read on.

Endnotes

[1] Gary Althen, *American Ways* (Yarmouth, ME: Intercultural Press, 1988), 13. According to Althen, involvement in community organizations and volunteer work are distinctive features of American culture that foreigners frequently find puzzling. As hosts, you may want to point this out and discuss it.

$$-5-$$

Cultural Baggage: What the Customs Inspector Doesn't See

Chances are you've already had the experience of being at the airport for the arrival of a colorful entourage of weary but wide-eyed exchange students. Although dressed in the usual teenage garb of jeans and T-shirts, their foreignness is rarely disguised; it is telegraphed by their uncommon gestures, their darting glances, the musical lilt to their voices, and their quizzical "Where am I?" stares.

As the students go through customs, the inspectors open suitcases, rummage through clothing, examine an occasional guitar case, and peer into packages and dog-eared cardboard boxes. Everything visible to the scrutinizing eye is checked. But there is something more that exchange students bring with them, something not so immediately obvious as highly visible suitcases, souvenirs, and flight bags. They also bring the beliefs, the attitudes, and the rules for proper behavior that they have learned at home. Each student's combination of these personal and cultural characteristics constitutes what we are calling "cultural baggage."

It is only after exchange students have crossed the threshold, unpacked, and stored their suitcases that this invisible baggage gradually begins to appear. Here are some of the ways invisible baggage becomes obvious:

In the middle of the night, a Mexican teenager named

Margarita awoke with the terrifying thought that her American host father was planning to seduce her. It turned out the father had given the teenager a goodnight kiss and hug—something he routinely did with his own children. He innocently assumed his behavior would convey to Margarita nothing more than fatherly affection. But Margarita did not think of him as her father and was not used to expressions of affection from males outside of her natural family. She considered his behavior inappropriate and threatening.

Another standard that differs from culture to culture is the attitude about what is considered proper attire, especially the way one dresses in casual situations around the house. An American student staying with a Colombian family was viewed by his hosts as indiscreet. "Robert didn't bring a bathrobe, pajamas, or slippers," contended the señora. "He'd sleep in shorts and just put on his trousers to go to the bathroom. I didn't like this."[1] Similarly, a student from Australia, Rachel, was accustomed to dashing about her natural family's home in a sheer nightgown: her parents thought nothing about it, since attitudes regarding nudity generally are more liberal in Australia, and nude bathing on some beaches is the norm. But Rachel's American family relied on a different (unspoken) dress code and felt quite embarrassed about Rachel's behavior. As a result of their embarrassment, Rachel's host father and brothers erroneously concluded that she was "flirtatious" and "seductive."

A Chilean exchange student found that his cultural baggage spilled out at the dinner table. "Ricardo was selfish," his American host mother concluded. "He would take two pork chops, and then the platter would be empty when it reached the last person around the table." Ricardo hadn't recognized one of his host family's cultural assumptions: one pork chop is the appropriate amount of meat, and when the platter contains one chop per person, taking more is considered greedy. Instead, he was still functioning as though he were with his natural family in Chile where *appropriate* was defined as the amount of food necessary to satisfy the appetite—whether that meant one or two or three pork chops per person. Knowing that, Ricardo's natural mother and the family maid always prepared enough pork chops to meet individual needs.

Ricardo's host family, on the other hand, based their definition of appropriate on the notion that meat is a semiluxury to be eaten sparingly. The host family planned their meals around this definition but never realized they should explain it to their exchange student.*

Food is particularly important in the hosting relationship, since it often carries a heavy burden of cultural meaning. Sometimes it is used to express hospitality. It can also express such things as love (giving chocolates on Valentine's Day), celebration (toasts with champagne), poverty (beans and rice are considered peasant food by some Brazilians), and appreciation (a gift of bottled herring!).

One American host family learned the hard way that certain foods also express contempt. When they served their German student corn on the cob, he stood up and left the table. Only after a long discussion was it clarified that for most Germans, it has traditionally been an insult to serve corn; in Germany, corn was until recently considered to be barnyard food.

A different kind of misunderstanding developed between an American host family and a student named Eduardo. He had concluded that his family was cold and boring, and the family had concluded that they had been sent a rowdy student who was making selfish demands that he be constantly entertained. "Eduardo wants the U.S. to be just a big party," his host father complained. Eduardo retorted by exclaiming, "This place is as dead as a cemetery."

In South America, Eduardo lived in a bustling city where an extended circle of family and friends routinely planned weekend visits to restaurants or gatherings at home, with lively discussions and dancing that lasted late into the night. In contrast, his host family lived in the suburbs, relatives were widely

---

* There are skills and techniques you can use to minimize and resolve cross-cultural misunderstandings. For suggestions, see chapters 10, 11, and 12 and appendices B and C.

dispersed, and contact was mostly by telephone. Evenings were spent watching TV or videos, while Sundays were special because the family could chat with friends after church.

With Eduardo and his host father each assuming (without conscious awareness) that his own culturally based way of socializing was "correct," neither could appreciate that one approach was just as valid as the other. Instead, each had spiraled into highly charged and negative conclusions about how one of them was "right" and the other one was "wrong."

Invisible baggage can also control the way one goes about disagreeing. In many American families, it may be the rule that outright confrontations and arguments with one's parents are unacceptable, but children are allowed to disagree by complaining and "talking their way out of" doing certain things they don't like. But in an exchange student's culture and family, the way that disagreement is expressed may be quite different.

If a Brazilian is unwilling to go along with a parent's request, instead of questioning "Why do I have to?" he will be more inclined to respond "Maybe" or "O.K., I'll do it later," and it's understood that he plans to do it never! Similarly, a Malaysian girl might disagree by saying "yes" verbally but saying "no" in her grimacing facial expression.

It's not that Brazilian and Malaysian teenagers never disagree with adults. It's that each culture has different definitions of the "respectful" way to disagree. Consequently, if cultural cues are misread, both sides can wrongly conclude that they are dealing with someone dishonest, irrational, or rude.

What each of the above examples portrays is the complex nature of cross-cultural interaction. Typically, each party is unaware that the other has a different set of unspoken rules for appropriate and respectful behavior: each has a different way of looking at the same situation.

What's more, it is the seemingly trivial or ordinary daily activities in the new culture that tend to cause the worst misunderstandings, with both host and sojourner feeling insulted and hurling blame. This phenomenon—trivial matters causing the worst misunderstandings—may seem paradoxical. After all, we normally defend the things we value and ignore matters that are inconsequential, not vice versa.

The key to understanding this apparent paradox is the following: while the triggering event may seem trivial, the underlying motivating cultural rules are not. After all, these are the rules which make it possible for us to live together as families and as nations. And when these "sacred" rules are violated, we react—sometimes quite negatively—for it's then that we have been hit by cultural baggage that we never even suspected was there.

Ray Gorden, a researcher who studied communication patterns during the homestays of Americans in Colombia, elaborates on this point:

> Often we tend to simplistically assume that misun-
> derstandings over "trivial matters" would not lead
> to any serious consequences between people of
> intelligence and goodwill. Yet, we have consider-
> able evidence that both the Americans and Colom-
> bians drew rather basic conclusions about the oth-
> ers' character as a result of "trivial" misinterpreta-
> tions. Few Americans realized that such "trivia" led
> the majority of Colombian hosts to conclude that
> their [students] were "generally thoughtless of oth-
> ers," that "they think they are superior," and that
> "they do not care about their reputation among
> Colombians."[2]

Just how much of our everyday behavior is influenced by cultural baggage, and how much will it affect the interactions you have with your exchange student? As one international sojourner muses:

> Cultural baggage is like "no-see-ums"—those
> nearly invisible little flying bugs that we Floridians
> have to contend with all the time. They're every-
> where and nowhere at the same time. Cultural bag-
> gage, too, is always buzzing around and often caus-
> ing a little sting.

Quite understandably, you will never actually "see" an ex-change student's—or anyone else's—cultural baggage. But we do become aware of it, at least indirectly, in the everyday behavior (and misunderstood behavior) that it produces.

Endnotes

[1] Raymond Gorden, *Living in Latin America* (Skokie, IL: National Textbook, 1974), 28.

[2] Gorden, *Living in Latin America,* 6.

—6—

What You Need to Know about Culture

When we Americans use the word *culture*, we usually mean one or more of the following:

> *High culture*: the performing and visual arts and formal etiquette.
>
> *Folk culture*: oral traditions, folk dances, songs, and proverbs.
>
> *Traditional culture*: our national anthem, holidays, songs, heroes, antiheroes, and monuments.
>
> *Popular culture*: fads, slang, pop music, movies, and magazines.

Careful thought reveals, however, that culture is much more. Culture, you see, does nothing less than shape our total way of behaving and looking at the world. All of this is governed by an elaborate system of rules, assumptions, and patterns of thought that we have learned, that we carry within us, and that we act on each day of our lives. This system—the one that dwells within our minds—is known as deep culture.[1]

Deep Culture

The internalized rules and assumptions of deep culture are like an elaborate, memorized guidebook. It tells us things like what is important (progress and the future) and what is not (inherited titles and royalty), what is right (hard work) and what is wrong (being unpatriotic). These rules and ways of thinking (and there are hundreds of them) are how and why we experience our culture subjectively—from the inside looking outward, not vice versa.

Here are some examples of deeply embedded cultural rules that you may or may not be aware of:

- White lies are acceptable if they save face and embarrassment and avoid hurting feelings.

- When talking with your boss, don't interrupt, talk loudly, or dominate the conversation.

- Don't call casual friends on Sunday mornings unless it's unusually important.

- When speaking to friends, don't stand closer than about two feet. (They aren't supposed to "feel your breath" when they listen.)

- If you're going to be late for dinner, call and explain why.

As you can see, we have all learned these rules, and they are stored away for our use. But we are rarely aware of them— they function on autopilot. Over time, we learn to simply *breathe the logic* and then to forget that we have ever even learned it.[2]

You will recall that in chapter 5, we described deep culture as the out-of-awareness "cultural baggage" that exchange students bring with them or, more accurately, within themselves. Now you know that we Americans also carry cultural baggage within ourselves and that much of our daily behavior is influenced by it.

To further explain culture's impact, let's explore five major areas which are shaped by a person's enculturation: perceptions, values, ethnocentrism, stereotyping, plus language and communication.

Perceptions

People in a given culture tend to view events in the same way without ever realizing that they hold common perceptions that differ from culture to culture. For example, when they watch

TV sitcoms, most Americans are attuned to the plot and jokes. But a foreigner watching the same American TV program for the first time may be attuned to the dubbed-in laugh tracks— a facet of the show Americans usually don't notice at all. Why does the foreigner notice what you don't? Because people see and hear in a selective fashion without realizing that they have been culturally conditioned to notice only certain aspects of any given situation.

Values

In each culture, people have their own common values about what is meaningful and important in life. When Brazilians remark that Americans are "work crazed and cold," the comment reflects the fact that their values about work, play, and what is important in life are different from ours. Such a comment also suggests that—without realizing it—they are looking at American behavior through Brazilian eyes. Of course, we Americans have our own culturally based definitions of what's right and of value. As a result, we sometimes criticize Brazilians as being "undisciplined and hedonistic."

Ethnocentrism

Once people have acquired the perceptions and assumptions of their own culture, they tend to become ethnocentric, unaware that there are equally valid alternatives and convinced that their way of life is the only "natural" and "reasonable" way for human beings to live. Distortions, faulty conclusions, and judgmental put-downs are the inevitable result. Why? Because by using one's customary point of view, unfamiliar behavior is viewed as being wrong, not just different. In time, a rigid belief system emerges that insists, "I am right, others are wrong," "Americans are superior, foreigners inferior."

By contrast, open-minded thinking says (1) there are many different ways of looking at the same situation, (2) to understand an event or behavior, it must be interpreted within the intended frame of reference, and (3) learning is a lifelong process of discovering new reference points and shedding one's ethnocentrism.

Open-minded thinking leads us to the realization that our American culture is one design for living among the many in the history of humankind. Ours is an adaptation to one environment, one level of technology, and one set of historical circumstances. Like all others, our culture is unique, but neither superior nor universal. We can claim superiority only if we size up other cultures by inappropriately applying our own cultural standards and values to their situations.

Stereotyping

Using generalizations is something everyone does. In fact, it's a necessary part of our everyday thinking because doing so helps us categorize into manageable chunks the barrage of stimuli constantly coming at us. Stereotypes evolve when we try to understand the behaviors of foreigners and in the process apply our own cultural rules and values, ending up with a distorted understanding. Over time, when enough people do the same thing, a stereotype is born which "just seems right" for describing every member of the foreign group. Yet in reality, stereotypes blind us to the uniqueness of each person and foster serious misunderstandings.

There are hundreds of stereotypes that we hold of foreigners and that they hold of us. For example, one of the reasons that the French consider Anglo-Saxons "inferior" is because smiling is so much a part of our everyday life. But not for the French. In lieu of smiling, French children are carefully taught to greet others with a respectful "Bonjour, madame" or "Bonjour, monsieur."* They learn this lesson well— so well that as adults, they conclude there must be something a bit "goofy" about people who merely smile instead of offering a polite "Good morning, madam" or "Good morning, sir."[3]

Equally unflattering is our stereotype of the French as being "rude." This view arises in part because American travelers do not find the French helpful when they ask for direc-

---

* The word *madame, monsieur,* or *mademoiselle* must be included as an indication of respect.

tions or advice. You see, Americans do not typically begin an inquiry for help by first saying, "Excuse me for interrupting you."[†] Precisely because of this omission, the French are offended by the American's "intrusion," and the American typically doesn't get the kind of helpful response he or she is seeking. And so the stereotypes persist.

It might be helpful to know that there are a number of common stereotypes which many exchange students recite when describing us. In general, we are seen as work-driven, generous, always in a hurry, boastful, lacking in human warmth, vulgarly materialistic, and obsessed with innovation.[‡]

A useful exercise might be to discuss this topic with your student and to identify stereotypes held by both sides. Such discussions not only allow you to see how Americans are misperceived when viewed through a foreigner's cultural lens, but they also allow students to understand us without necessarily liking all that we represent. From the host family's perspective, the discussions can serve to challenge the belief that Americans are perfect and *should* be loved by everyone.

Language and Communication

It is important to bear in mind that our conversations are more than just the words we speak. We also send silent messages, and the better we know a person, the more we can anticipate and interpret those messages. For example, when Dad fixes his gaze, clears his throat, and says, "William Henry Hawkins—you know what to do," and his son replies, "Gotcha, Dad," and heads for the kitchen, both parties are clear about what's being communicated although most of the message is implied. Dad doesn't have to say, "Billy, you know the rule. You

---

[†] There are situations where Americans are just as careful about the words they use. Among close family members, you might hear a "Pass the salt," but when the situation is more formal, the request *must* include "please."

[‡] Two commonly expressed generalizations about Americans are that we are ignorant about other cultures and that we suffer from a superiority complex. Many Americans would concede that these generalizations are, unfortunately, true.

must take out the garbage on Sunday nights. That's your job, and it's one of the ways used in this culture for teaching you to be *responsible*."

Billy understands his dad's shorthand because both of them are relying on deep culture, which gives meaning to their verbal and nonverbal messages. Mr. Hawkins conveys higher authority by fixing his gaze and clearing his throat, signals social distance by using Billy's formal name, and evokes the cultural rules that apply to the situation. Few spoken words are needed because of the silent language[4] provided by their shared cultural conditioning; both have this second, silent language well memorized.

The nonverbal and implicit messages that we convey are part of what is known as context. Without a context that is shared, there is no particular meaning to the words we speak. The lack of a shared context is the villain when foreigners complain, "Americans seem to laugh when I say something serious and don't laugh when I tell a joke. Why is that?"

What we are saying is that language, like just about everything else, comes drenched in culture. Could this throw a monkey wrench into things from time to time? Yes, indeed, because with your exchange student, you will lack a shared cultural context and this deficit could trigger misunderstandings. Look how this deficit affected one Japanese girl and her American family:

It was Hiroko's very first dinner with her American hosts, and they were serving apple pie. The evening itself was a big occasion for her, and the dessert in particular represented a special treat. Hiroko excitedly and with much anticipation watched as a generous slice was cut and passed to her. Quite suddenly, however, she declined it. As a good Japanese, Hiroko had been taught to be "polite" and to say "No, thank you," for she knew she should accept only after the treat had been offered several times, but her American hosts did not know this. Also being "polite," they never thought to offer it to her repeatedly.

What this poignant example teaches is this: one may hear the actual spoken words but miss the overall meaning. That's because Hiroko and her American hosts lacked a common cultural context. And the result? A very disappointed Japanese student and a bewildered host family.

To communicate across cultures, families must recognize that a shared cultural context is lacking, that this deficit can—at times—create a barrier, and that they must compensate for it. To do so requires the use of special intercultural communication skills, one of which will be discussed shortly. Using such skills creates a bridge between deep cultures.

If Hiroko's American hosts had known about deep culture and bridging skills, they would have searched for the rule which explained her behavior, the Japanese rule of self-effacement. It goes something like this: When honored with praise or an award, do not show pride or express entitlement. The proper demeanor is one of humility. If you are offered a gift, refuse it to show you are not deserving. Accept gifts only if there is profuse insistence.

Seen in this light, Hiroko's response was entirely appropriate because she felt honored and presented with something special. Her words were a self-effacing token, not an expression of refusal. Had her hosts only known this, they surely would have insisted that this special new person in their lives accept the long-awaited pie.

The "Noise" of Deep Culture

It may surprise you to learn that these kinds of misunderstandings and even serious communication breakdowns occur with some frequency between exchange students and their host families. Even more surprising may be the fact that these problems occur not by accident. They are often a reaction to a breach of our embedded cultural rules.

As we mentioned earlier in this chapter, deep culture typically functions silently, on autopilot, but when its rules are broken, that's when the silence ends and the "noise" begins. This noise frequently reaches its highest pitch when people from different cultures converse and interact. That's because they lack a shared context, a shared deep culture, so they are repeatedly violating each other's norms. As you can imagine, this rule breaking can occur frequently between hosts and their exchange students. Complaints such as "Geraldo's a liar" or "Ana's such a slob" are examples of the noise you might hear.

Quite possibly, the noisy vocabulary of clashing cultures will sound familiar to you, but to help with its identification, listed below are some typical comments to watch for. If you notice more, add your own to the list:

Spoken by the host family:		Spoken by the exchange student:	
He's selfish.	He's immature.	That's stupid.	That's crazy.
She's spoiled.	He's a brat.	That's disgusting.	They're snobs.
He's rude.	He's egotistical.	They're boring.	They're cold.
She's greedy.	She's lazy.	They're dense.	
She's dressing like a tramp.		They're too old to understand.	

At other times this "noise" has no words at all; it just erupts as strong emotion directed at a target: being shocked by, feeling used by, or laughing at (rather than with) your student.

Watch for Red Alerts

It's not hard to see that the noise of deep culture is frequently composed of emotionally charged comments which distract and interfere. Still, these comments can serve a positive end. They can be viewed as powerful signals warning of cultural barriers ahead—proceed with caution! We have labeled these tip-off reactions as "red alerts."[§] By identifying them this way, you can spot them in conversations and stop, reflect, and investigate for cultural differences.

For one seasoned host family, it is a feeling of irritation that puts them on red alert. They explain why they pay attention to this signal and how they use it to solve problems.

> When Siri does something that we find irritating, we go into the cultural education mode. This means telling her what has bothered us and pointing out how her behavior is contrary to our cultural pat-

---

[§] See Appendix C, "RADAR to the Rescue," for a complete explanation of red alerts.

terns.[II] If we ignore the signals and just tolerate
the behavior, our anxiety/resentment/anger starts
to build. Eventually we just explode. And guess
what? The student is the target.

Granted, it can take exceptional maturity and understanding to handle these situations well, and you may not always
be successful. But it is important to make the effort, for reasons the family quoted above explains.

First, we can't expect our student to be a mind
reader. Second, when Siri does not know—cannot
know—that her behavior is irritating us, she will
just continue it.

Our advice to families is this: by keeping your
antenna out, watching for red alert signals, and
going into the cultural education mode, it's a sure
bet that you can prevent cultural differences from
creating big communication barriers. Make it happen. You'll be glad you did.

In Summary

"Culture is a mold into which we are all cast."[5] Culture shapes
our personalities, regulates our behavior, and gives us a shared,
comfortable worldview so that our lives have meaning and
value. We simply couldn't survive without culture.

But truth be told, we all get a bit too much of its instruction. Just like the athlete who overtrains and becomes muscle-
bound, years of cultural training rigidify our mental and emotional muscles, leaving us with "hardening of the attitudes."
We can become inflexible and culture-bound. Years of
enculturation also tend to make us ethnocentric and prone to
the habitual use of stereotypes and bias. Moreover,
enculturation can instill a craving for what is familiar and correct, promoting a narrow "right-wrong" mentality which

---

[II] The family acknowledges that there are also times when its student has
red alert reactions and will ask for a discussion of cultural differences
and family rules.

causes us to fear differences and to react strongly to change. We can be blinded to other worlds and even to new ideas and novel possibilities close at home.

Perhaps the previous chapter and this one have been your first exposure to the deeper, subjective level of culture. If so, you may be ending this section feeling like a fish in the sea which has been swimming along unaware of its aquatic condition. Now you may notice a first-time-ever awareness of feeling "wet," not to mention surprised, and perhaps even a bit shaken. You might even go so far as to call it a form of culture shock. Coming face-to-face with culture can be unsettling, but increased cultural awareness is good.

It is our hope that as you reflect on your own heritage and perhaps challenge some of its rules, you will become less culture-bound. Breaking free of its limitations can be quite liberating, possibly leading to something like this:

> I recently read an article, "Bowling Alone,"[6] which presented a very gloomy forecast. The author said that Americans are participating in fewer group activities—including bowling leagues—and because of this change, our civic pride is on the decline and with it the potential demise of our American Way of Life. It seems like bowling alone is a signpost on the road to catastrophe!
>
> There was a time when I was frightened by such predictions. I thought that change was bad—that change meant breaking old rules with awful consequences—that I would be in big trouble if I didn't behave exactly as society expected. What if I slurped my soup at a formal dinner party? Would everyone gasp and stare at me? Would I end up with a second-rate spouse in a second-rate marriage? Would I be an embarrassment to my employer and friends?
>
> As I have matured, I have learned that the world will not inevitably come crashing down about my ears if I make cultural mistakes. If I accidentally slurp my soup, I will not be fired, nor will my

spouse desert me. I have even come to realize that soup slurpers are the norm in Japan.

My fears were based on pressures that we all feel to conform. The truth is, there are many ways to live. I have learned that difference and change can be positive—they are not necessarily to be feared.

In the next couple of chapters, we will describe some situations in which both families and students react with discomfort when their cultural rules and assumptions are challenged. As hosts, it is important for you to know that these strong reactions are a normal part of the overall experience. Moreover, it is important to realize that challenges to deep culture can be very beneficial—they often spark important eye-openers. Whenever possible you will want to respond, not with defensiveness or blame, but with understanding and insight (see chapter 12 and Appendix B for specific strategies and suggestions).

As you give consideration to this advice and the overall message of the chapter, we hope you agree with Mary Alvey, an exchange organization official, when she says,

In the end, we must all accept the fact that hosting is not just family entertainment; there is built-in stress and discomfort. But with knowledge, good preparation, and tolerance on everyone's part, the experience can be successful, enjoyable, and provide valuable learning opportunities for everyone involved.[7]

Endnotes

[1] Edward T. Hall, *The Silent Language* (New York: Anchor/ Doubleday, 1959).

[2] Raymond Carroll, *Cultural Misunderstandings: The French-American Experience* (Chicago: University of Chicago Press, 1988), 47.

[3] Polly Platt, *French or Foe? Getting the Most out of Visiting, Living and Working in France* (Culture Crossings, 1995).

[4] Hall, *Silent Language.*

[5] Ibid., 52.

[6] Robert D. Putnam, "Bowling Alone: America's Declining Social Capital," *Journal of Democracy* 6, no.1 (1995): 65-78.

[7] Personal communication, 1996. Mary Alvey is a regional director for one of the major youth exchange organizations. She also speaks from personal experience; she has been involved with teenage exchange for over two decades, and her family has hosted close to thirty exchange students.

—7—

The Adolescent Sojourner's Experience

Just as all of us have our ups and downs in life, so do exchange students, although their ups may be a little higher and their downs a little lower. After all, they are international sojourners who have temporarily left behind everything familiar—all while going through the turbulence of adolescence.

It should be emphasized that there is not a set of experiences through which all students go. Nevertheless, there are many experiences which are common among them and certain stages through which many, if not most, of them pass. Highlighting these may help you better understand the challenges of hosting. In later chapters we offer very specific, practical suggestions for helping your exchange student through the stages of cultural adjustment.

Arrival Fatigue

Newly arrived exchange students are often at the peak of an emotional high. There have been months of preparation, a long flight across international borders, and the thrill of meeting their hosts for the first time. The family, fueling this excitement, begins making immediate plans to do and see everything.

In many cases, it isn't long before the student begins looking glassy-eyed, yawning drowsily, and responding only halfheartedly, causing the family to feel confused and mildly insulted. "Sure, he's a little tired from traveling," the family acknowledges, "but if he really wanted to, he could overcome it and enjoy being here."

What families might not realize is that their student has arrived physically, but that is about all. On the inside, many students feel "lost in space" and mildly miserable with the symptoms of what we have called arrival fatigue. Jet lag and all the newness have caught up with them. Although they have been welcomed into an American home, they might sleep more than usual or pace and fidget, feeling lost in a collection of new and disconnected experiences.

Some students are understandably a bit nervous, perhaps remembering a previous occasion when, surrounded by unfamiliar people, they did not quite fit in. They might worry that they will never get over the initial discomfort of not knowing what to say, especially in a new language. How will they make friends? What if they find their host parents too strict? What if they do not understand their teachers? Also, how will they cope with the fact that they are already missing their families and close friends?

In addition, exchange students often succumb to language overload that comes from straining to understand and speak English. As one student put it, "I thought I would scream if I heard one more word of English. It felt like bombs were going off in my head." Communicating becomes a little like trying to converse under water: people may be talking, but what comes through is a mere babble of gargles and gurgles. "I would try to understand," a student notes, "but the words just flew past my head."

Along with fatigue, the newly arrived student is subject to stimulus overload or underload. Students from what could be considered highly demonstrative cultures (Latin, Mediterranean, Arab, etc.) are used to activity—lots of it: talking, gesturing, and touching. For them, life in the United States can be like going from the city to the country; they may feel like it is "too quiet," even though there is much that is new and much to be learned. On the flip side, for students from less demonstrative cultures—less activity, more pauses in speech, fewer gestures, less touching—it is like going from the country to the city; initially they can feel overwhelmed by all of the "comings and goings."[1] Whichever the case, it is unsettling until an adjustment is made.

Dealing with so much so fast is exhausting, and it is the combination of the changes and newness that results in arrival fatigue.[*] It will last, understandably, about as long as it takes to recuperate from the travel and to become familiar with the new surroundings. Some students will have only a few mild symptoms, which begin to disappear within a few days. When students start school immediately upon arrival, the fatigue might last for a month or more. Eventually, when they recover and learn enough to move about with some ease, optimism usually surfaces.

Settling In

Rather than focusing on the differences between life at home and life in the new culture, it seems that sojourners initially pay more attention to the comforting similarities. Consequently, an exchange student soon recognizes that in certain ways, Americans are just like everyone else: they eat meals, work, shop, study, watch TV, and drive cars. "Everything is just fine," a student might think at this point. Of course, some superficial cultural differences might be noted, but with a bemused "How interesting" detachment.

As students get their bearings, many notice discrepancies between what they expect from their sojourn and what is, in fact, reality. Overly positive expectations come in many guises, sometimes causing students to hope they have found "perfect" host parents or will have a family experience that is tension-free and brimming with boundless affection.

---

[*] The exhaustion from speaking a new language coupled with stimulus overload or underload is also sometimes called *culture fatigue*.

Another unrealistic expectation is that their foreignness will automatically transform them into special people who will be showered with attention in the classroom and enthusiastically embraced by the popular kids. When they are at times received with disinterest or even ridicule, they can become crestfallen and disillusioned.

The glitter of Hollywood feeds still another faulty expectation. Since many exchange students are influenced by the way Americans are portrayed in TV and movies, they at times erroneously expect their host families to live like flashy celebrities who own lavish mansions and have wisecracking kids like those on television sitcoms.

Exchange students from large cosmopolitan centers sometimes encounter surprises of a different kind. They expect to find compact towns and cities that bustle with activity, especially teenage discos and nightlife. More importantly, they expect their host communities to have modern rapid transit systems. They are not prepared when they find themselves in a sprawling suburb, a slower-paced small town, or a tranquil farm community without convenient public transportation or friends to get them places.

To help dispel these kinds of unrealistic expectations, many families begin a correspondence dialogue with their student several months prior to arrival. As one host father explains,

> We don't wait for a sponsoring organization to call us saying they have a student and can we take one. We make the selection several months in advance, going through many applications looking for very specific characteristics and strengths. We exchange letters, faxes, e-mail, and pictures as part of a get-acquainted process to develop realistic expectations. We want to build a bridge between one family-living experience and another, to offer an invitation into our lifestyle and hearts, and to reassure the natural family that their teenager will be in the loving care of a responsible family.

By the time our student arrives, we're head and shoulders above the rest. Yes, we go to a lot of work, but isn't it worth it? Don't we all want to max our chances for success?

Deepening the Relationship

As noted, students eventually reach a point of feeling some uncertainty about what to do, how to behave, and how to relate. Their own deep culture rules become inadequate as guidelines. This is a period, then, in which they will be fumbling, testing, exploring, and experimenting. Relationships develop as the family clarifies its lifestyle and begins the important process of explaining American cultural patterns.

Culture Shock

The stage is set for culture shock when the thrill of the arrival fades, dreams become frayed at the edges, and the sojourner stops saying, "This place seems so much like home."

What is culture shock? Let's begin by clarifying some things that it isn't. Culture shock is not life threatening. It's not a medical condition or even mildly related to the rather severe medical condition of "going into shock" from physical trauma. Nor is it something to be particularly alarmed about. In general, the words *culture shock* describe a major learning experience that sojourners go through.

There are at least two factors that bring on culture shock. One is the new cultural environment, the external factor. The sheer number of changes in the lives of sojourners can compound their sense of frustration as they struggle to accomplish a simple task. Much of what they see strikes them as erratic and senseless. Quite often, their customary way of thinking can produce confusion rather than understanding, and their usual behavior might look unacceptably strange and out of place. All of these frustrating and confusing and overwhelming differences cause culture shock.

Sometimes what is overwhelming and perplexing in the new environment is a harsh, sudden encounter with the host culture's expressions of ethnocentrism and prejudice. A Polish exchange student, Mikolaj, living with his host family in New Jersey, mentions this painful experience.

> When American students told ethnic jokes and said cruel things about the Polish immigrants, I could not believe what I heard. I was shocked and speechless. I was hurt by that badly. Most of the bad experiences came from the lunch period. I just couldn't stand to be there.

For Mikolaj, culture shock came at him hard and abruptly and was the result of a specific environmental stimulus, but bear in mind that sojourners can also have forceful culture shock reactions which, ironically, are triggered by their own inner experiences. Here is what we mean: people living abroad have strong reactions when they begin to really think about the notion of culture—that is, deep culture, and what it is all about. It dawns on them that there are other ways of life which they don't understand, and that the seemingly self-evident rules they were taught as children are not "absolute and sacred" after all—the rules can be arbitrary, they can be broken, they can be different. A surge of awareness occurs and with it a psychological jolt. Sojourners are caught off guard and are shaken to realize that they are just now learning about something so pervasive, something that has affected them every day, all of their lives. They feel strangely naive, vulnerable, self-conscious, and often frightened as they come face-to-face with this profound discovery.

When they look inward, sojourners confront the cultural facts of life—and the facts can be "shocking." It's like an internal earthquake. The psychological awareness that life is vastly different somewhere else—that there are other, equally valid sets of cultural rules—causes their entire deep culture superstructure to tremble and sway uneasily while it is being reorganized.

When all this happens, a sojourner may find it difficult to function well. Distress can—quite understandably—cause exchange students to behave in unusual ways, to have emotional swings or even upsetting thoughts. Some students become concerned about cleanliness and begin to bathe or shower repeatedly. Others might become preoccupied about sickness or safety. If your student smokes, he or she may smoke more often. Overeating is common, although some people lose their appetites almost completely or worry a lot about weight changes. Missed menstrual periods, insomnia, and oversleeping can also occur. Emotional reactions can include withdrawal, irritability, or moodiness.

Researchers aren't sure why, but some people never experience culture shock at all. Those who do experience it may recover in a matter of weeks or months, but some take a year or longer. A few students never fully adjust to the new culture and end up only marking time until they can return home. A small percentage may suffer from extreme culture shock symptoms[†] for such a long time that an early return home is the best solution.

Because of the wide variety of reactions to culture shock, we can't predict exactly what will occur for any particular student. However, the general patterns that we are describing should be helpful. Here are five major features.

Identity Concerns. Travelers to foreign countries can have a hard time figuring out what is going on. Consequently, it might seem to your exchange student that Americans laugh at the wrong time, get excited about trivial matters, ask embarrassing questions, or don't know how to express friendship even if they are always smiling. That's because the two cultures have different cultural rules and scripts for defining when it is appropriate to laugh, what events are meaningful and should arouse an enthusiastic response, what topics are too private to discuss, or how to convey respect and make friends.

[†] Guidance regarding severe symptoms is provided in chapter 15: "Taking Stock." Practical suggestions for helping with normal culture shock behavior can be found in chapter 13: "Culture Shock."

When students do not know what to do or when to do it, their sense of self-confidence and identity can be shaken; in fact, students sometimes feel so confused that they wonder who they really are. As one student declared, "My host family doesn't know who I am, and neither do I."

Atypical Behavior. When culture shock begins, host families sometimes wonder if someone switched students on them. That person who was so charming and outgoing can turn sullen or cling like a frightened child. It can be quite disturbing to try reasoning with someone who overreacts, underreacts, makes harsh judgments, isn't logical, or has scaled the pinnacle of stubbornness by insisting absolutely, "I'm *not* going through culture shock!"

Anger. When confused and frustrated, sojourners often find it comforting to put the blame on someone or something else, and the closest targets are you, the host family, and the new culture. After all, things were fine until they arrived on foreign soil, so blame oozes out in the form of complaints and irritability. "This culture (or country, or place) is awful," reasons the student, "because it makes me feel awful." The counterpart to a student's intolerance for the new culture is constant or exaggerated praise for one's home culture. "My country's way of doing things is so much better," the sojourner might boast. In a few cases of culture shock, sojourners reject most aspects of the culture they have left behind and "go native." "Because everything in the U.S. is so wonderful, I'm going to become an American," they insist.

Incidentally, at this stage it is often useful to hold discussions which stress this important point: the new culture doesn't have to be viewed as good or bad, just different.

Homesickness. The very nature of being an exchange student means leaving behind all those things one dearly loves—parents, home, friends. Quite understandably, many students experience sadness, and some retreat to their bedrooms or become noticeably moody.

However they go about it, most students need some time for feelings of loss. This is normal, making it possible for sojourners to free themselves emotionally from their home culture and temporarily find comfort in a new place.[2]

Recovery. As culture shock subsides, the sojourner becomes less judgmental and more accepting of the differences between the home and host cultures. When this shift occurs, cultural differences are no longer seen as good or bad; they are viewed as opportunities to learn something new.

Recovery, however, is rarely sudden. It is generally a slow process, punctuated by minor declines; just when everything seems back to normal, the sojourner might come up against some new problem which causes the confused feelings to return momentarily. Inevitably, as your student learns more about American culture, life in your home won't seem so strange. (For detailed information about culture shock, see chapter 13.)

The Holidays

Students on year-long exchange programs almost always arrive in the United States just before school begins in the fall. Three or four months later—maybe just when they are emerging from culture shock—the holiday season arrives.

For people coping with stress, it is generally well known that the holiday season can be troublesome, so it is not surprising that for many exchange students, the holidays bring a longing for family and friends and an awareness of being an outsider in the midst of merriment. Even students who have barely felt any culture shock symptoms might feel wistful and subdued when everyone around them is bustling with holiday preparations.

Of course, many students thoroughly enjoy the holidays with their host families. Furthermore, those whose important celebrations fall somewhere else on the calendar may be less likely to feel additional pressures.

Taking Stock

After the holidays, many sponsoring organizations hold midcycle orientations to encourage students and hosts to evaluate how the experience is going. This is a time to reassess goals and expectations as well as to address any lingering adjustment difficulties. The latter could involve prolonged or extreme culture shock symptoms, troublesome rivalries within the family, difficulties at school, or problems making friends. For most, the stage is brief and prepares the way for significant new learning.

Culture Learning

Students start learning about their host's lifestyle and about American culture the moment they arrive, but an in-depth exploration of cultural differences often gets delayed until culture shock passes and major adjustments have been worked out. That's when a period of culture learning begins.

Many host families report that going through the culture-learning stage brings about the most enjoyable experiences. The long talks that were necessary to explain family rules and routines now give way to easy conversations and good times together. A deep friendship often develops as each makes new discoveries about the other. As one host father explains,

> It's not like someone throws a switch and we're suddenly close, but after four or five months, we notice a remarkable difference: there's a comfortable family affection, a sense that this kid belongs here…in our family…with us. I'd ask myself, "Was there ever a time when Eve wasn't here? It just feels like…forever."

Predeparture

As the end of the homestay experience approaches, a mixture of feelings may emerge: enthusiasm about farewell parties and graduation activities, apprehension about saying goodbye, excitement about returning to loved ones back home, concern about having changed so much that acceptance at home will be difficult, along with doubts about whether others will understand how one person could be in such a state of confusion. Here is how one student expressed his ambivalence.

> I'm going back. I can hardly wait, but what's my
> Mom going to look like? Will my sisters be taller?
> What if I speak with an American accent? Will my
> friends accept the new me? Will my American host
> family still love me after I've left and am far, far
> away?

As hosts, you will want to be aware that it is not at all unusual
for students to protect themselves by emotionally distancing
themselves from their host family. This can be seen through
behaviors like withdrawal, irritability, and faultfinding. For
more details, see chapter 17.

Readjustment

Upon returning home, sojourners typically surge to another
emotional high—a euphoric peak that comes from being re-
united with family and friends. Yet, inevitably, the student
notices that much has changed—perhaps the returnee most
of all. So once again, the "Who am I?" questions emerge, leading to another emotional slump which is known as reverse
culture shock or re-entry shock.

As with culture shock, reverse culture shock creates feelings of disorientation and anxiety. Only this time, it is the
student's home culture, natural family, and friends which are
the sources of discomfort. There can even be homesickness
as the student longs for a family—in this case, the host family—which has been left behind.

Experts say many students find reverse culture shock to
be the bumpiest part of the entire exchange experience. Eventually, most students can agree with a student who said,

> In the United States I crossed hard times and diffi-
> cult understanding. My culture shock was more than
> a word, but I had a wonderful American family. They
> loved me like their son, and I loved them back.
>
> I didn't think all this could happen in such a
> short time. I never laughed or cried or learned so
> much. In the United States I became a man with
> myself; I went there to get my adult, and I got it.

Endnotes

[1] The United States is considered to be a relatively low-demonstrative culture. However, Germans, the German-Swiss, and Scandinavians are considered even lower. Edward T. Hall, *Beyond Culture* (New York: Anchor/ Doubleday, 1976), 79.

[2] A. C. Garza-Guerrero, "Culture Shock: Its Mourning and the Vicissitudes of Identity," *Journal of the American Psychoanalytic Association* 22, no.2 (1974): 422-23.

—8—

The Host Family's Experience

You now know that exchange students face a kaleidoscope of new experiences. As they confront this vast new world, they see things that are interesting and perplexing and shocking.

It may seem a bit strange to consider, but people can stay at home—in their own culture—and still go through certain phases of culture shock, especially when they are challenged to think about their own cultural heritage. We have called this parallel experience "retroshock"* because it is the backward glance at their own culture that prompts the reactions.

Retroshock can occur when people move into an ethnic neighborhood and get closely involved, fall in love with a foreign student while in college, or sponsor an immigrant family—to name a few of the many triggering events. In such situations, the intimate encounter with someone different prompts them to look back—to re-examine aspects of their upbringing, their beliefs, their accomplishments, or their points of view. Richard Brislin, a researcher and professor, has studied this kind of contact. His ideas are summarized as follows:

> As any close friendship develops, there is a sharing
> of personal thoughts and experiences, an accep-

---

* The authors have coined the word *retroshock* to reify the host family's experience. Retroshock is differentiated from culture shock or reverse culture shock. The latter typically occurs when sojourners return to their home cultures.

tance of each other's admirable qualities and faults. In cross-cultural friendships, there is also a growing awareness of vast differences in outlook and values. If we try to really understand and come to terms with the differences, we inevitably realize that it is culture that has shaped those differences. This new awareness can provide us with an actual first-hand encounter with what is meant by "culture," an encounter that transcends a mere textbook understanding of the word.[1]

The same is true of host parents for whom a long, close relationship with a young person from another culture can provide powerful opportunities for learning, so that if a student's ideas appear shocking or if his or her questions challenge fundamental beliefs, intense feelings can be stirred up, bringing the host's way of life and identity into question. Furthermore, the host parents may feel dismay or disillusionment if there is a loss of cultural innocence or an increased awareness of deep culture conditioning. More specifically, here is what it can be like:

Retroshock: a mild to moderately upsetting condition experienced by families who host foreign exchange students; a disturbance of the family's routines, composure, outlook, and convictions. Although not as intense, it is the family's parallel condition to the exchange student's culture shock.

Symptoms: irritability, feelings that range from delight to discouragement, and a loss of objectivity.

Time of Onset: early in the hosting experience when families are surprised by their own reactions. Or when the family seems to "catch" a mysterious affliction which influences or "contaminates" its outlook and beliefs.

Antidote: relaxing with the idea that going through retroshock is a normal part of being a host parent and entering the experience informed and prepared.

One host mother experienced retroshock as an emotional high. Being an opera singer who loved Japanese art, she became enthralled by her Japanese exchange student's exquisitely delicate, porcelain-like face: "I would see Michi enter the room and have a wonderful feeling of being connected with centuries of living Asian art."

Families who host Middle Eastern students might have a mild jolt before the morning coffee has been perked. One host mother who got up early to prepare a special breakfast for the family recalls the following embarrassing moment:

> I'd just started cooking when Abdul walked in, got a whiff of the bacon and blanched. In a curiously repelled voice he asked, "What's that smell?" After five minutes of ghastly silence, it dawned on me: Muslims don't eat pork. I thought, "Oh my gosh! I know that. Why didn't I think of it?"

In another situation, a host father swung by the house one weekday afternoon to pick up some business papers. As he dashed by the kitchen window, something on the back lawn caught his eye. It was his Swedish exchange student, Inge, sunbathing entirely in the buff. "Now *that* took some adjustment!" exclaims the host father, his eyes widening with laughter.

> When I walked into that situation, I ended up doing more than saying, "Hey, get some clothes on, Inge." I was hit really hard by the clash of cultural standards. I began to consider the whole notion of what's decent and why.

There was no chagrin at all for Inge, because in her culture it is quite normal for women to sunbathe topless at home and in public parks, but on that sunny spring afternoon, this particular host father was suddenly hit with the reality that our American standards are far from universal.

In addition to giving you a reality jolt, having an exchange student in your home can start some reminiscing. Things your student says or does may trigger a flood of old memories, awakening feelings of nostalgia for what "might have been," as one mother recalls.

Having Yuko in my life and home forced me to look back and say, "Gee, I wish I could have been like this Japanese girl. I would never have had the courage to get on a plane and step off in a new world, unsure of whom or what I would encounter. To have that kind of faith in yourself and take that kind of leap is simply…wonderful!

As a teenager, I was very shy and never ventured outside the boundaries of the world I knew. So I missed many opportunities. I am now determined not to miss many more. I've told myself, "I'm not going to *not* do something because I'm afraid of making an idiot of myself. I'm going to take the chance, take the risk." It would be awful to die without having done the things I want to do, just because I was afraid to try.

Hosting Michi, Abdul, Inge, and Yuko prompted eye-openers which encouraged the hosts to learn more about themselves and to acknowledge that influence is not all one-way. Children influence and mold their parents, and by the same token, exchange students influence and mold their hosts.

Certainly, experiences like the ones presented above can cause host parents to look back—to revisit their own adolescent years, to question aspects of their lifestyle, to compare cultural traditions, and to understand things from a totally new perspective. In the process, families can begin to feel exposed and sometimes find their beliefs somewhat shaken. Exactly how retroshock comes about in the hosting experience is explained next.

A House of Mirrors

To stay afloat in the stormy waters of life's compromises and complex realities, adults often drop anchor in protected harbors. They adopt a policy of ignoring, tolerating, and excusing. Teenagers come along with their youthful zest and exaggerated idealism to rock the boat of parental complacency and occasional "sellouts." They sometimes interrogate their parents with intimidating questions about topics adults would prefer to ignore.

When parents try to reform their kids but inevitably exhibit imperfections themselves, their teenage children may ask,

- Why do you think drugs are worse than your cigarettes or coffee? Nicotine and caffeine are more addictive than marijuana.
- You go to the gym to get exercise. So why do you drive two blocks to the convenience store?
- You make a big deal out of recycling, but you use paper plates.

Teenagers, as you know, can be deadeyes for adult hypocrisies and foibles. They stand opposite us, raising to our faces a life-sized mirror which reflects back our frailties and forces us to look and see ourselves as we really are.

How might the "adolescent-as-mirror" phenomenon affect the hosting experience? Your own children are likely to comment on your lifestyle contradictions; exchange students are likely to draw attention to both your lifestyle contradictions *and* your cultural contradictions. So, inviting a teenage exchange student into your home can multiply the mirror phenomenon tenfold. Almost nothing that is said or done will escape scrutiny. Not only can you as a host parent be gently nudged into acknowledging your personal flaws and inconsistencies, you might also find yourself floundering when your views are solicited about politics, thorny social issues, or American cultural values.

You may not find an easy answer or a quick escape when asked questions such as the following:

- Since the United States has only 12 percent of the world's population, why do you consume nearly two-thirds of the earth's natural resources?
- How can you spend so much money on pet food when there are homeless people on the streets?

- Did you both get jobs just so that you can buy those expensive shoes that your ten-year-old bugs you about? Who's in charge here, you or your children?[†]
- How can you call this a classless society when you rank first among prosperous nations in the inequality of income?

Some veterans at hosting say that these kinds of questions can seize you by the scruff of the neck and give you and your values a thorough shaking. To endure and grow from such questions, it helps if

- you have cast your beliefs not in stone but rather in something a little more flexible;
- you can tolerate critical comments without arguing, apologizing, or trying to convert others to your way of life;
- you welcome the opportunity to examine what you stand for and why; and
- you delight in exchanges with adolescents because you enjoy their intensity, their candor, their rambunctiousness, and their questions, which can effectively turn your home into a "house of mirrors."

Loss of Cultural Innocence

Most of us can recall when we first learned there was no Santa Claus, or discovered where babies come from, or lost a grandparent. Each time we had one of those experiences, we were losing a bit of our childhood innocence. That innocence initially served a critical purpose: it protected us from biological and psychological realities which—if presented too early in life—could have been overwhelming and harmful. As we matured physically and emotionally, we gradually shed our

---

[†] As a cultural adviser, you may wish to discuss this major trend: "affluenza." Working parents are giving children more input in purchasing decisions. The result is a $147 billion "kid-sized" market in which parents face "threats of tears and taunts if their kids don't get in on the latest fads." AP article in the *Orlando Sentinel*, 5 September 1995, G8.

innocence and in exchange gained the knowledge and understanding that made us self-reliant and responsible adults.

While growing into and through adulthood, we also typically lose our innocence about social and political issues. We
are disturbed to learn that some doctors perform unneeded
operations, some parents abuse their children, some police
can be bribed, and some clergy abscond with church funds.
We are disappointed to discover that politicians who seem to
have strong ideals can operate cutthroat election campaigns
or that juries can convict innocent people on occasion. Of
course, we can blind ourselves to these realities. Or we can
acknowledge them—ugly as they may be—and grow wiser
and more tolerant (or at least more prudent) about whom we
choose as our doctors, ministers, and authorities.

Not always, but very often, bringing a foreign student into
the home can stretch one's loss of innocence another giant
step, exposing family members to international realities that
go far beyond the immediate family, community, culture, and
nation.

You might never have given much thought to the havoc
wreaked by World War II, only to receive a German teenager
who feels deeply guilty and affected by the Nazi atrocities to
the point of being embarrassed to be a German—even though
she, herself, is two generations removed from the conflict.
Yours might be a deeply religious family, only to have a teenager who belongs to a religion you know nothing about, who
has no religion at all, or who is strongly opposed to religion.

You might abhor the idea of sodomy, yet have your family
learn that it is quite acceptable and may even be widely prac-
ticed in some cultures. You might want your children to learn
the value of money—making them work for their allowance—
only to host a student whose family has built up fortunes beyond belief by supporting exploitation and oppression. Or,
you might have heard people say the United States has the
world's highest standard of living, only to encounter a Scan-
dinavian student whose country far exceeds the United States
in certain areas of health care, social services, and per capita
income.

Of course, you might not have any of these experiences, but each is a real-life example. Plus, almost every exchange student will say or do something at some point which has the effect of setting off some tremors within one's deep culture. An American host mother describes what happened to her:

> Being persecuted for one's Jewishness was just something I'd read about in a history book. For me, it didn't happen to real people. Then we had Jorge, an exchange student from Argentina. His grandparents had narrowly escaped being gassed in a Nazi concentration camp, and their story had been told and retold by the family.
>
> Jorge relived these horrors in frequent nightmares. My husband and I were shocked to see his pain, so we suffered, too. When we gave him a Star of David pendant for graduation, we thought he'd feel proud, but Jorge wasn't. "My parents have forbidden me to wear this. It's not wise for Jews to be marked, to be singled out in this way," he advised us.
>
> Seeing the living history that tormented Jorge forced me to participate in a deeper knowledge. No longer could I be a mere bystander to history.

We would suggest that you seriously consider what it might be like for your family to lose some cultural innocence. It might mean discovering that some of your treasured and long-held beliefs about the United States and other countries are only as solid as a sand castle lapped by ocean waves. Hopefully, any such retroshock experiences will produce positive changes similar to those described by this host mother.

> Before we hosted a student, we were in the dark ages about our family, life in the U.S., other cultures, and America's impact on the world. We may not do any better on geography tests, but our view of the world has definitely changed. I don't think we could ever be persuaded that one way of life is categorically right. We've lost our belief in incontestable, absolute, singular opinions. We've moved into a world with a hundred shades of gray in it, and for us, there's absolutely no backing up from that.

How Long Does the Family's Retroshock Last?

Experienced families say there is a good chance that retroshock will start out mildly, intensify two or three months into the homestay, and then begin to ease up . By the midway point, few symptoms may remain, but to some extent, it will probably be around as long as there is an exchange student in your home.

"At first everything was perfect, but after we'd had Juan awhile, the honeymoon feelings vanished," states one host mother who began to notice things that were either surprising or upsetting. A host father occasionally found himself "fed up" and began asking, "Why did we make this decision? What am I getting out of this experience except aggravation?" Explains a third host parent:

> When things suddenly aren't wonderful any longer, that's usually a sign that the family has entered a period of intense learning and adjustment. It helps an awful lot if the family understands what's happening and can see the benefits of it.

How much or how little a host family experiences these reactions will depend somewhat on family members and how deeply they want to get immersed. Some may desire only a quick dip. Others may feel challenged to take a deep, exhilarating plunge. If you want to temper or slow down your learning, mention to your exchange student that you prefer not to discuss sensitive topics or debate cultural differences for a while. Also, try to schedule shared activities (trips to museums, craft fairs, sports events, special celebrations, etc.) and deemphasize lengthy or deep discussions.

On the other hand, if a personal growth experience is what you want, you may find that both phenomena—the "house of mirrors" and your "irreversible loss of cultural innocence"— have enriched your life.

Rewards for the Family

Host families frequently believe that the principal value in hosting is the opportunity to share their home and lifestyle with someone from a distant land. As one family put it, "As

Americans, we have such abundance, so why not share it?" It was only after their student had returned home that this family realized that something unexpected had happened, that they, themselves, had been significantly changed by the experience. They had become more attuned to world issues, more mindful of their own enculturation, more cognizant of how people tend to see events from their own cultural perspective, and more sensitive to the idea that each culture's way of life is equally valid. Heightened awareness and "dual vision" had dislodged them from being 100 percent Made-in-America.

People who share these kinds of broader cross-cultural perspectives and experiences constitute what might be called a global culture. No longer immersed in a single culture, they are linked to a larger international community.

It is our hope that this book will help you relate to an exchange student in such a way that it serves as your passport into the global culture, enabling you to leave behind the security of the known and journey into new, exciting, and challenging cross-cultural dimensions.

Like many families, you may be contemplating hosting a student for the first time, you may already have a student, or perhaps you are considering repeating the hosting experience. Your motivation may be one of many. Maybe you want to experience or re-experience the sense of deep accomplishment that comes from making a positive contribution to a teenager's development. Maybe you want to expand the horizon for your own children and help them learn to live with diversity and change. Maybe you want to examine or re-examine your own values and lifestyle. Or maybe, like the mother quoted below, you like the idea of becoming hooked on hosting.

> The first time you try it and like it, you realize just how much you've been missing. So, of course, you want to do it again. It's as if you've been led into a bountiful orchard of tempting, new experiences. You can't resist reaching for one more because they are just waiting there, ready for the picking.

Endnotes

[1] Richard W. Brislin, "The Benefits of Close Intercultural Relationships," in *Human Assessment and Cultural Factors*, edited by S. H. Irvine and John W. Berry (New York: Plenum Publishing, 1983), 536.

Part II

Hosting Guidelines
and Suggestions

—9—

The Hosting Stages

> Our Little Bundle of Joy will be arriving in two weeks, so we will be host parents to a bouncing new sixteen-year-old once again. Yes, we have a name...Julia from Amberg, Germany. Actually, this is one of those miracle births, as her host mother weighs only slightly more than the new arrival and will maintain her weight after birth. Personally, we are looking forward to the experience with much anticipation.

Like this proud host father to be, you too may be awaiting the arrival of an exchange student. If you have children of your own, perhaps you remember how, in those months and weeks before you became a parent, you searched for books and asked other parents for advice that would help you meet the new challenge of child rearing. Now as you face the prospect of hosting, you may be looking for the same kind of information and practical guidelines to prepare you for what's ahead.

To provide this kind of guidance, in the next nine chapters we discuss the various stages of the hosting experience and examine some of the typical features of each. We give you some ideas about what to expect at different points in the homestay and also suggest some recommendations on how to handle day-to-day situations.

The nine stages of hosting as portrayed in the diagram below are these:

1. Arrival
2. Settling In
3. Deepening the Relationship
4. Culture Shock
5. The Holidays

6. Taking Stock
7. Culture Learning
8. Predeparture
9. Readjustment

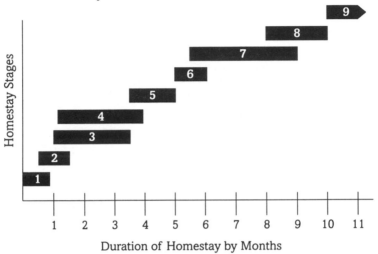

Duration of Homestay by Months

As you spend the next few months with your exchange student, we hope that this framework will give added meaning and structure to events. If at some point you begin to suspect that adjustment roadblocks have developed—for either your student, family members, or both—you might find it helpful to refer to the stages to determine what may be causing the difficulties. In these situations, try not to blame your student or yourself. Instead, talk the matter over, and if appropriate, seek constructive help from the sponsoring organization.

Remember, too, that the model we have developed will not describe every situation. All models are somewhat hypothetical, and there's still only limited formal research available about the host family's experience. While hosting experiences vary in length, we have somewhat arbitrarily chosen to base our model on the popular ten-month format. If your student will be living with you for a shorter or longer period, you may find the stages somewhat condensed or expanded.

In addition, some organizations place students with different families over the course of the program, either because families prefer a shorter commitment or because problems emerge in an earlier placement. Exchange students who have already been in the United States for a while, whether in your own community or another, will have gone through some of the earlier stages of adjustment, but they will still face a new adjustment to your family. For guidance with these situations, we suggest you consult the sponsoring organization.

Finally, as you read the next chapters please keep in mind that it's our intention to offer suggestions rather than to specify what must be done. If you have previously hosted a student, you have your own experience by which to judge the usefulness of any given suggestion. If you are new to hosting, then we have provided signposts for an experience that we hope will enrich, if not change, your life.

$$-10-$$

Stage One: Arrival

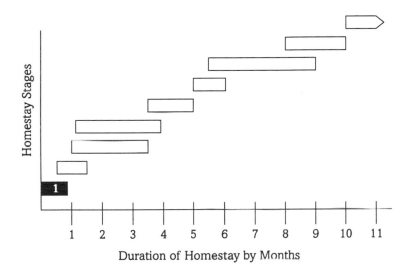

Stage One begins the day an exchange student arrives* and usually ends before the one-month mark. Typically it lasts from seven to fourteen days.

---

* We have not described the period before the student's arrival, since many families are not recruited very far in advance. However, when families receive the name of their student several weeks prior to arrival, an important bonding process can begin through the exchange of letters, faxes, e-mail, and phone calls. Through these contacts, both the family and student begin developing realistic expectations of the other. And, equally important, feelings of caring and interest begin to grow.

When visitors arrive at the doorstep, we greet them enthusiastically to let them know they are welcome in our home. But for exchange students, greetings can be awkward. Not only may your student be confused by a handshake or misread your hugs and kisses (if this is not how greetings are expressed in his own culture), but he may also be too weary with arrival fatigue to appreciate your expressions of hospitality.[†]

While your gestures of welcome might be overlooked and your words misunderstood, undoubtedly your concern for the student's adjustment will be appreciated. As one host mother notes,

> Of course I always smile and shake hands when I first meet our exchange students. But I try to put aside the idea that doing so means a whole lot. Instead, I do all I can to help that exhausted and confused kid regain his confidence and get his bearings. That's what's important. That's the best welcome.

Thus, without ever saying so in words, your thoughtful and comforting actions can convey a message of welcome: "You're with people who understand what you're going through and who know how to be helpful."

To assist you with this kind of practical welcome, we have put together a number of suggestions. Tackle the first set during the initial days. Later, when your student is a bit more settled, go through the second group, but keep this in mind: in these first few days and weeks, it's just humanly impossible for you as hosts to explain everything that your student needs to know. Likewise, it's humanly impossible for your student to learn and understand everything immediately. So mistakes and awkwardness and fumbling are going to be unavoidable— on both sides. Try to accept it, relax, and focus on these essentials:

[†] Beginning in this chapter, we will use the male pronoun for general references throughout an entire chapter and then switch to the female pronoun in alternate chapters. But whatever pronoun is used, the example will always apply to both sexes, except for references to specific individuals.

- Your student probably needs rest.
- You will need to provide a short orientation fairly immediately.
- Make sure your student knows that you are available for help and to answer any and all of his questions.
- Be sure to explain that in your household it is okay to make mistakes.
- Take care of the arrival tasks and issues (as described below).

Topics for Immediate Discussion

Safe Arrival Communiqué

Contacting home within twenty-four hours of arrival is usually of primary importance. In so doing, students reassure both their natural family and themselves that all is well. They also re-establish an all-important bond with their parents[1] and calm inner fears about being so far away. Most students will want to telephone, fax, or e-mail their parents very soon after their arrival. If the telephone is used, it is completely appropriate and, in fact, recommended that the call be made collect or with an international phone credit card. Also, if you haven't done so already, now is a good time to write a note to your student's parents. Briefly introduce your family, tell something about your lifestyle, and express your thanks for the opportunity to share their son or daughter.

Jet Lag and Health Concerns

Long international flights and layovers—combined with changes in time zones, weather, food, and water—can leave a student exhausted. Encourage naps and expect irregular sleeping and eating patterns. Ask about stomach upsets, especially diarrhea or constipation, which are likely to be embarrassing and uncomfortable topics for your student to mention. Be prepared to offer medication or advice just as you would with your own children. Be supportive of your student's recuperation by pacing exposure to new experiences and minimizing overstimulation. Remember that initially a student's attention span may be short; plan welcoming parties and outings in accordance with signs of recovery.

You should also inquire about any prescription and non-prescription medications your student may use. (Sometimes this information is omitted from application papers.) Girls may need help soon after their arrival in buying tampons or sanitary napkins but are likely to feel awkward or lack the vocabulary to explain their needs. Have some supplies available and be clear about how to dispose of these items. A little bit of embarrassment now is better than dealing with plumbing problems later.

A related concern that worries some girls is that they experience delayed periods as a result of the stress and dislocation of travel. Your reassurance that this is a common occurrence should help ease their concerns.

Silence and Conversation

Americans tend to be talkative, especially among strangers. In a crowded supermarket line, we will strike up a conversation to appear "friendly" because we feel awkward and asocial if we don't fill up the time with something. Talking (especially "small talk") is our way of being comfortable among strangers. As we get to know a person, we tend to talk less. So the rule with Americans is: the greater the intimacy, the greater the ease with silences.

We mention this because when your student first arrives and you feel somewhat awkward around him, you may want to talk almost nonstop. Your student may be expecting just the opposite pattern: silence initially and continuous overlapping talk as the friendship warms up. Be sensitive to the possibility that you both could start drawing some wrong conclusions and feel mildly uncomfortable or possibly even offended.

Personal Space, Privacy, and Property

Bear in mind that personal space, privacy, and ownership may be defined differently by your student in his own culture. He may be from a culture where all members of a family freely use household items, which for them are considered common property. American exchange students living with families in other countries are sometimes shocked by what they misconstrue as a disregard for their personal possessions and privacy as, for example, when a Thai host brother or sister eagerly opens the suitcase of a newly arrived American exchange student and studies its interesting contents.

Your exchange student probably won't make exactly the same assumptions as you do about what is personal and what is meant for use by the entire family. American host brothers and sisters sometimes take offense when their exchange student walks right into their rooms without invitation or uses their CD player without asking permission. Yet your student may not understand that he has done anything wrong. For this reason, it is a good idea to be fairly specific about personal space and property.

Orientation to Your Home

Showers, toilets, faucets, appliances, and electronic equipment sometimes work differently in other countries, so you will want to make sure your student understands how to use these various items. But accomplishing this can be a bit tricky. You don't want to explain something that your student already understands, thereby insulting or embarrassing him. After all, your student's own shower or toilet may be more sophisticated than yours.

It's best to approach each item by asking something like this: "What, if anything, looks different about our bathroom?" From the response you get, you will know whether a specific demonstration is called for. As you continue through the orientation, keep using similar questions: "What is the same here, and what is different?" Not only will you discover what your student already knows and what you need to teach him, but you will also learn something about your student's culture and show that his customs are of interest to you. This will set the stage for future cultural learning.

Your Student's Bedroom Area

To help your student feel comfortable in your home, on his bedside table place a "Welcome Kit" containing airmail stationery and stamps (or aerograms), a small telephone directory with important numbers, a house key, a three-by-five card listing family members' names and your address and phone number, and a small bilingual dictionary. Invite him to display photos and mementos which can help personalize the room and remind him of his cultural heritage. "We buy a teddy bear for each girl," says a couple that has hosted several students. The bear is placed on her bed, with a note that goes something like this:

> They told me you were coming. I'm so glad you're
> finally here! I hope you will give me a name soon.
> I'm really looking forward to being your best friend.

Family Bulletin Board

If your family has a central "command center" (for the family calendar, various schedules, school lunch menus, phone messages, and the like), you will want to point out this area to your student. He will also be part of this system, with his own set of meetings, rehearsals, sports practices, and telephone calls. It is a good idea to post mealtimes, when people get up, evening curfew hours, and so on.

Decisions about Names

It is often difficult for exchange students to decide what to call their host parents. You may appreciate this problem if you recall the difficulties you may have had in coming to a decision about how to address your in-laws. Some students and families reach a decision to use first names even though it is understood that the adults are more than peers. Others jointly decide that the adults are to be addressed as "Mom" and "Dad."

Incidentally, some students are bothered if you ask them to call you "Mom" and "Dad" because they conclude that by using words which imply familiarity and closeness, you are asking them to forego the strong ties that they have with their natural parents. That's why we suggest that this topic be openly discussed, that you make sure the student doesn't think you're expecting him to fit in like your own child or attempting to replace his real parents. This isn't an issue with all students, but the important thing is to discuss the matter and to make sure that a misunderstanding doesn't develop.

While discussing names, ask your exchange student if you are pronouncing his name correctly and if the name you're using is the one he prefers. If your student's name is difficult for Americans to pronounce, develop a phonetic pronunciation and write it on a card which can be shown to people; for example, Caio (KY-you) rhymes with "MY-you."

Sometimes families like to give their students an American name or nickname, either because the student's real name is difficult to pronounce or because this is their way of expressing affection. If you wish to do this, again we suggest you discuss the matter. Some students feel that calling them by a new name is an insult or a threat to their identity. Others like it and feel flattered by the attention.

Pets

You may think of your dog Sparky or your cat Dinah as quasi members of the family, but your exchange student may not be accustomed to being around pets, especially inside the home. He may be uncomfortable when Sparky jumps up and sniffs him or is allowed to lick the plates after dinner, when Dinah is found taking naps on his bedroom pillow, or when your own kids talk to these pets and kiss them. In some cultures, dogs are viewed as unclean, and religious codes prohibit them from being touched. Others consider dogs as food. With this wide range of attitudes, you will want to use caution and discuss the issue of pets early on.

Family Prayers

If your family is religious, it will be important to discuss those practices that affect daily life in your household. Before including your student in family prayers, especially mealtime blessings, explain what will transpire and ask if he wishes to participate. Sometimes nonreligious students choose to participate because they like being involved in all family activities, though they may not share religious beliefs. But keep in mind that your student might feel uneasy and even threatened if expected to be involved in unfamiliar religious rituals. Here's how one host family handles this sensitive area.

> It is fundamental that no two people hold exactly the same beliefs, even those who sit in the same pew or kneel together on a rug as the call to prayer is issued. So why not widen our prayers to embrace all those at our table?
>
> As hosts, we tell our student, "We will make room for you, please make room for us. We are Christian. We pray before our meals, and we will mention you in our prayers.... You may also wish to offer a mealtime blessing. If so, please include us in your prayers.
>
> "We do not want our prayers to make you uncomfortable. It is not our attempt to convert you to our ways. However, prayer before meals is important to us. We hope you will respect this and understand our spiritual needs. We will do our best to understand yours."

Topics for Later Discussion

Once your student seems to be making an initial adjustment, there are numerous other topics you will want to cover. When doing so, try to be mindful of cultural differences, and whenever possible, use the bridging skills which are presented in Appendix B. A few topics for later discussion are presented below.

Personal Hygiene

In some cultures it is customary to shower several times a day. So you may find your water bill soaring unnecessarily if your student comes from certain tropical regions and continues this practice here. Also, American families sometimes need to encourage the use of deodorants with students whose standards may be different. And some girls are accustomed to using more perfume than American teenagers, while some boys pour on aftershave lotion. Regarding such differences, it is good to keep in mind that each culture has different definitions about what is considered "clean," what are acceptable body odors, and what are acceptable fragrances.[†]

Regarding fragrances and odors, be aware that your student may be uncomfortable with some "hidden odors" in your household. For your student, these unpleasant odors could come from foods you eat; your different ways of cooking; the use of room deodorizers and cleaning products; cigarette smoke; perfumed dried flower arrangements; pet smells; and litter boxes. Household changes may not be practical, but be aware that your student might be trying to adjust to things you simply take for granted.

Language Fatigue

Keep in mind that even with years of classroom language training, speaking English continuously can be nerve-racking and exhausting for a newly arrived student. To make matters worse, many students notice a temporary decline in fluency. Consider creative solutions to communication barriers: draw pictures, try acting out what you want to say, and post signs around the house to label items like "oven," "hair dryer," and so on.

During these first weeks, students make dozens of language errors. We suggest you ignore all but those which are likely to get him in trouble or laughed at.[§] Since comprehension may be low, you may need to repeat or rephrase your sentences several times. For important matters, ask your student to repeat back what you have said, because it is too easy

---

[†] Even we sanitized and deodorized Americans have offensive odors to some cultures. Asians who don't eat dairy products sometimes say that Americans give off an odor of milk. Similarly, Hindus, who eat no beef, sometimes complain of an unappealing smell.

[§] For suggestions to help with language learning, see Appendix A.

for him to just nod and agree with you when he is generally overwhelmed.

Mealtime

Table manners and food preferences vary from culture to culture. Naturally you will want to be sensitive to foods that the student might avoid for religious reasons, and, in general, you should not expect your student to like everything you prepare. Many food tastes take years to acquire, so don't take it personally if you discover that your student is avoiding one of your specialties. Just as many Americans do not eat snails, insects, dogs, octopus, or horse meat, likewise foreigners often find our food preferences strange or even disgusting.

When food is passed around the table, it is often a good idea to encourage family members to go first so that your student can see what the appropriate portion is and how foods are eaten. If at first your student does not participate wholeheartedly in mealtime conversations, remember that speaking in English can be stressful and exhausting. Also, some cultures—and some families—discourage conversation during meals.

Safety Concerns

While you don't want to frighten your student, you will want to discuss with him the potential dangers that face adolescents and what to do if he encounters problems. Discuss the importance of locking doors, how to handle phone calls from strangers, how and when to answer the door, the dangers of accepting rides from strangers, places to avoid, and so on. Make sure that your student knows the evacuation route from your home in case of fire, and make sure he knows how to call the police, fire department, or ambulance in an emergency.

Community Orientation

During the first couple of weeks, introduce your student to important places in the community. Experienced host parents say it's best to go slowly; they try not to visit more than one place per day. Some likely destinations are the local post office, a bank where he can cash traveler's checks or perhaps open an account of his own,‖ the closest convenience store or pharmacy, and the school. Your student will probably not be allowed to drive while on the program, which can be a bit inconvenient in many suburban or rural locations. However, he will need to be able to direct other drivers to your house, so try to help him identify the key landmarks quickly. Other locations of likely interest are the public library, the mall or main shopping area, or a music store where he can buy cassette tapes or CDs. The supermarket may also be fascinating at first.

U.S. Money

While almost everyone is at least somewhat familiar with U.S. dollars, your student may not know the denominations of our coins. He may not expect the sales tax that is added to his purchase, or understand when he needs to leave a tip or how much. Many students will need help budgeting their funds and learning how much their U.S. money will buy, especially if they find the prices here are less expensive than at home. They may be tempted to buy everything they ever dreamed they wanted.

School Registration

You should plan to help your student with registration for classes even if there is an adviser assigned by the school to assist him (school enrollment should be prearranged by the sponsoring organization).# Some schools or exchange programs require that exchange students take certain prescribed

---

‖ Veteran host families recommend that students open a savings account from which withdrawals can be made. Checking accounts usually involve monthly fees or minimum balances.

Many private schools also welcome exchange students and often waive tuition. In addition, some schools organize their own programs in which students and/or faculty are exchanged.

courses. But when the choice is up to the student, you might want to encourage him to enroll in classes like journalism, chorus, current events, and so on, where there is more opportunity for conversing and making friends.

Schools usually have policies stating whether foreign students can participate in varsity sports, receive a diploma, or hold senior standing. Many give students the opportunity to purchase a class ring and a yearbook, grant an honorary diploma or certificate of attendance, and invite them to take part in graduation ceremonies even though requirements for graduation have not been met. In any case, clarify these matters now so your student does not develop false expectations.

For your student's first days of school, try to find an American student (possibly your own son or daughter) who is willing to act as a guide—helping your student get to the right bus, find classes, figure out how to work the lockers, make it through the cafeteria line, and so forth.**

In Summary

In these first days of hosting, remember that you are laying the groundwork for a successful experience. For your student, despite the jet lag and bewilderment, there may be moments that make a lasting impression. This was the case for Jeff, an exchange student in Japan, who learned a great deal on his very first day at school.

> As I sat eating lunch, several inquisitive Japanese guys, thumbing through dictionaries, eagerly crowded in, peppering me with questions. When three of the boys started looking things up with unusual seriousness, I instantly thought that I was about to be asked a difficult question about U.S.-Japanese trade relations, or maybe differential calculus.
>
> Finally, they closed their dictionaries and se-

** For more information about American high schools and the teenage subculture, see Appendix A under the heading "School Adjustment."

> lected a spokesman. I was still organizing my
> thoughts on U.S. foreign policy when the spokes-
> man asked, "Jeff, which girl in this class do you
> think is the prettiest?"

Jeff had always assumed that boys' interest in girls was "a fundamental part of human nature," but because of stereotyping, he had never quite extended his thinking to the Japanese.

> It struck me that until then, I'd never even consid-
> ered the possibility that a Japanese high school boy
> would think of anything except his schoolwork. In
> all my time in Japan, I think the most valuable les-
> sons I learned were that high school boys chase
> high school girls, and that mothers force their chil-
> dren to eat vegetables. It seems pretty silly, but
> perhaps significant, that I had to go all the way to
> Japan to learn that.

Endnotes

[1] Robbins Hopkins, "Defining and Predicting Overseas Effectiveness for Adolescent Exchange Students." Ph.D. dissertation, University of Massachusetts, 1982. This research suggests that successful sojourners have good communication and a close relationship with their natural parents.

—11—

Stage Two: Settling In

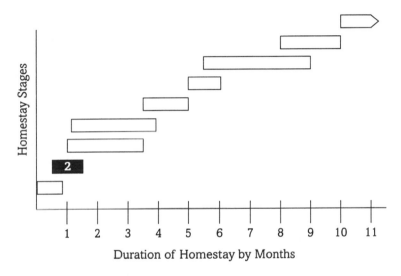

Duration of Homestay by Months

Stage Two begins as early as the second week and can extend to the seventh week. Typically, it covers about a five-week period.

Parents come in many varieties, but most have this in common: they have learned how to adjust to the changing needs of their growing children. As a parent, you learned to adapt to 2:00 A.M. feeding schedules; you had to cope with your teenage daughter's getting acne and PMS and hogging your makeup mirror; and you hardly even flinched when your fifteen-year-old son grew overnight to six feet and his shoe size surpassed thirteen. No doubt you were at times terrified about bumps and scrapes, illnesses and accidents, learner's permits and first dates; but despite the ups and downs, you got through it. You adjusted.

Hosting means carrying family adjustment one step further because now you have a slightly larger family. There is a need to settle into a compatible living arrangement and to develop ordinary routines. Few host families do this quickly and smoothly. Most find it awkward. In fact, there can be some "letdown" feelings as minor difficulties arise and reality sets in. One host father aptly caught the spirit of Stage Two when he suggested, "Things will be going just right, when they start going a tad wrong!" Indeed, a good adjustment has its rough spots—for you and your student.

On the pages that follow, three "settling in" experiences are described: (1) disruption of familiar family routines, (2) noticing imperfections in your exchange student, and (3) setting realistic goals. With any luck, our suggestions should help when things start "going a tad wrong."

Disruption of Familiar Family Routines

You say you're starting to miss those comfortable grooves of daily living? We suspect that another person is now tying up the bathroom, and another person's TV preferences must be considered; there are new concerns about privacy, seminudity, and displays of affection; there's someone else competing for telephone time; another person is making midnight raids on the refrigerator; and additional teenagers and neighbors are stopping by for impromptu visits.

With all these changes, families grow weary of the once-dazzling international person now living in their midst. One host mother expressed her shift in feelings this way: "When Pascal arrived, he just walked in and sat down in our hearts. We thought, Oh! This is just the perfect match. Now nothing seems to be matching."

As with this host parent, losing your "at-home" feeling may cause you to react with disappointment—even irritation and resentment—despite the fact that you fundamentally like the idea of hosting.

Your children might have some reactions, too. They'll probably understand that an exchange student needs extra attention, but this also means there's less time for them. In addition, any loss of privacy might be resented (especially if a bedroom or study area is shared), and sometimes there's uneasiness about all the attention that friends, relatives, and teachers shower on an exchange student. When these disturbances and changes occur, your children may react with insecurity, expressing feelings of jealousy, possessiveness, and rivalry.

For some families, the disruption of familiar routines is not very significant. For others, the changes seem major. Either way, it may help to know that you can begin to regain comfortable "at-home" feelings by developing new patterns and adapting old routines. Bear in mind that your student will at the same time be trying to adjust to your routines and searching for her niche in the family. Here are some suggestions.

Tune In to Your Routines and Rituals

Take time to carefully explain how things are done in your household, but first you'll need to become aware of your own routines. Sound confusing? If you're like most families, you're probably blind to many of your family patterns; they just function automatically. As one host father put it,

> You have to stop yourself in midstep, to consciously pay attention to the everyday things you do and to think about how your student is reacting to what you do. None of this is easy, but it's essential. One thing's for sure, you can't expect to explain your family's ways or expect your student to adjust to your ways until you yourself first realize all the little things that you are doing and that you are expecting from other family members.

Devise New Routines and Be Specific

Jointly discuss any accommodations that need to be made. Try not to accept a casual, simplistic solution like, "Hey, we've got a morning traffic jam in the bathroom. Everyone's got to get in and out faster!" Instead, work out a specific solution.

For example, some families designate a particular time for each person, possibly scheduling some showers for the evening. You might also consider moving some activities out of the bathroom, such as drying and styling hair or applying makeup, which only require a good mirror and perhaps an electrical outlet. Even something a little unusual, like an extra set of toothbrushes and toothpaste by the kitchen sink, could mean fewer bodies competing for the same crowded space.

While working out satisfactory new routines, encourage all family members—as well as your student—to be flexible and willing to compromise.

Expect Some Irritability and Resentment

Whenever routines are disrupted, some irritability can be expected. As an adult, you will be inclined to recognize the source of any grouchiness and not blame your student, but your children may not make this connection so readily. Before they take out their frustrations inappropriately, help them understand that their irritation is with the changes and not with the person.

Even though your love for your children has not diminished, the time you have available to share with them probably has, and your recently arrived exchange student needs your attention perhaps more right now than your own children do. If you sense your children's resentment and jealousy, take some time to discuss these reactions with them. While showing respect for their feelings, help them understand that lifestyle sharing involves both losses and gains. Perhaps with your help they can understand that change—even positive change—can make them temporarily feel insecure.

Temporary discomfort: these are the key words to remember. After about three to six weeks, you and your family should begin to feel a returning sense of comfort.

Noticing Imperfections

Before an exchange student arrives, host families generally don't know much about the person with whom they will share their lives and homes. In the absence of complete information, families sometimes start an embroidery process by mentally creating an exchange student who is perfect in almost every respect. These embroidered "dream students," fictitious though they may be, often come in handy during the first awkward days and weeks. That's because when little is known and communication is strained, embellishments can provide some needed comfort.

How will you know if you have fashioned in your mind some version of a dream student? Typically, dream students are expected to be flawless beings without bothersome imperfections. Some host parents try to turn their own untidy and grumpy children into angels by pointing to their newly arrived student as a model of perfection with inbred happiness. There is even an occasional host parent who anticipates that a student will compensate for the teenage experiences he or she never had. This may mean the student is expected to be one of those super kids who wins all the awards at school assemblies and sets the pace for the popular crowd.

Of course, as firsthand information accumulates, it usually turns out that the student does not have a halo and is not a carbon copy of perfection. "You begin to see the warts," as one host mother puts it. She goes on to point out that removing a student's halo isn't really all that bad.

> I think families eventually have to accept that hosting is not going to be a wish fulfillment. Exchange students are not perfect and angelic like Hummel figurines. They're normal, ordinary kids who make mistakes, break things, hurt your feelings, get upset and say things in funny ways—just like your own kids.

> Fantasies are a lot of fun, but a fantasy won't teach you anything new, and it definitely can't give you a hug when you've had a terrible day.

Setting Realistic Goals

Along with developing an accurate image of your student, it is also important to consider your goals. People almost always set goals (which in turn create expectations) when they want to accomplish something. Even with something so routine as our morning shower, we want to come out feeling clean and invigorated. But what if we enter the shower with fanciful expectations, somehow hoping that the pounding spray will enlarge our biceps or slim our waist? Then, no matter how invigorating the shower, we are likely to walk away feeling somewhat disappointed.

Likewise, to be successful with hosting, you need to set realistic goals—goals that you can, in fact, reach. In previous chapters, we've described some that we think are attainable: (1) hosting an exchange student for the purpose of lifestyle sharing; (2) entering the experience with a goal of learning about cultures (your own and others); (3) becoming host parents with the hope of developing a friendship with a person from another culture; and (4) wanting to expose your own children to cultural diversity so that as adults they can work effectively in a global community. Here's what one family has to say.

> When we took our first exchange student, we didn't give much thought to what we wanted to get out of it. Our neighbors did it, so why not give it a try?
>
> Now we go into it with clear expectations, and it's something we discuss. We tell our student, "We've invited you here to show you American life, but we are also doing this for our own personal enjoyment, our own learning. And if from all this there's increased international understanding and peace in the world—now that's a nice bonus!"
>
> We've seen families take a student to save their marriage, to provide a friend for their shy daughter, to get a live-in babysitter, to teach religion, or to sell democracy. When students are taken for these kinds of reasons, the family can be programming itself for failure.

If you have not already done so, perhaps now is a good time to think through what you hope to gain from the hosting experience. Talk with other experienced host families about their expectations and discuss with them whether or not your goals seem attainable. Also consider the following two suggestions.

Compare Goals within the Family. Make a list of your reasons for hosting and invite other family members to do the same. Use this as an opportunity to discuss and compare expectations. You might learn, for example, that your son isn't interested in developing as close a relationship with your exchange student as you are. This information can help you to be more tolerant should he choose to involve himself more with his own group of friends.

Discard Inappropriate Goals. In the process of sorting out expectations, you may discover that certain goals are best met in other ways. For example, someone who has taken an exchange student primarily to learn a foreign language might decide that the student can't really provide language instruction.

In the end, arriving at realistic goals means setting aside unattainable dreams and fixing your sights on what is truly possible. This process of defining and even redefining goals may occur not just once but quite possibly at several points during the year, and each time you may find yourself learning more about yourself and developing your capacity to adjust. As one experienced host father remarks,

> The kids and host families who seem to have the most problems are the ones that are not able to adjust their hopes to reality. Rarely is the exchange as we first pictured it. It is usually different in some significant ways. For it to succeed, we are forced to make adjustments. Very often, what we find is that things are better than we had hoped, even though they are different than we had imagined.

—12—

Stage Three:
Deepening the Relationship

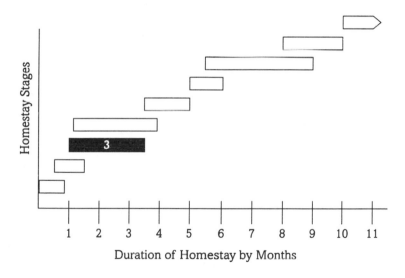

Duration of Homestay by Months

Stage Three begins at approximately the one-month mark and continues until around the middle of the third month. Typically it covers about ten weeks.

"Walk the talk." We've all heard the phrase. In business, it translates as "putting into action what you advocate in words." For host families "walk the talk" means moving beyond the token statement, "Yes, we want to have a good year with our student," to actively doing all that you can to make sure things turn out that way. One host father expresses it this way.

About six weeks into the hosting experience you realize, hey, if we want our exchange student to really understand our lifestyle, we've got to make it understandable. And, if we really want this person to be important to us, we've got to talk about the things that we actually do consider important.

You just come to a dead end and realize you can't continue on as before. You have to turn the corner and say, I'm going to do whatever it takes to make this a real-life, person-to-person adventure.

"Make your lifestyle understandable." What exactly is this father getting at? What exactly do you discuss? Certainly, there's a lot of ground that can be covered, but one of the most important topics is rules.

Household Rules

You may never have given it much thought, but it's your family rules that keep your household running on an even keel. Everybody knows and accepts and follows them, and they provide daily structure to your lifestyle. Granted, sometimes rules are viewed as negative because they get linked to punishment or restrictions, but that's a much narrower definition than we want you to consider. By and large, if you want your student to understand your lifestyle and what's important to you, it's essential that you present and explain how your household works.

Exactly what are your important household responsibilities and agreements and how can you begin to identify them? It helps to start by looking at the difference between stated or spoken rules and what we call *expectations*, which are most often unspoken agreements.

A small number of your guidelines are spoken—rules that you verbally explain and stand behind. "Only one hour of TV on school nights" might be the rule in one family. Another family might not say anything about how long the children can watch TV but will insist on "no snacks before dinner" or "only fifteen minutes per phone call." Some families try to keep rules to a minimum and say, "We have only two rules: Be honest and show consideration to other family members. For everything else, use your own judgment." Regardless of the number of spoken rules, family members can usually recite them, and they know the consequences if the rules are broken.

What we seldom realize is that the majority of our family patterns are governed by unspoken rules—expectations—that are rarely discussed or even thought about. These silent rules are frequently a reflection of culturally based assumptions about what constitutes appropriate behavior, and they constantly influence our thinking and actions. Here are some examples: "Family members should always volunteer to help each other and not wait to be asked." "When upset, girls in the family may cry; boys are allowed to get angry and occasionally swear." "Never eat the last piece of cake without first offering to share it." "If Dad falls asleep while watching TV, don't change the channel!"

Among the culturally based unspoken rules, there are certain topics that almost all host families need to discuss so that misunderstandings don't arise. These topics include (1) how we express appreciation/thanks in our family; (2) how we express disagreement; (3) what it means in our family to be "on time"; (4) when and where (in the house) teenagers can entertain their friends (for example, many European teens entertain in their bedrooms. Is that okay in your home?); (5) the meaning of a shut and/or locked bedroom door (I'm angry, I'm resting, Don't bother me, I'm thinking); and (6) appropriate bathroom etiquette and hygiene.*

---

* Of all areas in the home, the bathroom generated the most misunderstanding for American exchange students living with their Colombian hosts. Because household rules and expectations were rarely discussed, Americans and Colombians both falsely concluded that the other was "unclean," "inconsiderate," and "arrogant." (Gorden, *Living in Latin America*, 37.)

You'll want to discuss these matters so that agreed-upon behavior patterns are established. You've done it with your own kids. Now you'll want to do it with your student. However, talking with your own kids is one thing. Talking with an exchange student is different. In fact, it's very different.

Don't Use Rules to Americanize Your Student

As a parent to your own children, you have taught them proper behavior and household procedures, enforcing the rules and expectations with discipline when necessary. By establishing procedures, like giving your daughter the task of taking out the garbage, not only is she helping out with the household maintenance but you are also preparing her to be a good U.S. citizen because "working as a team" and "being responsible for a job" are valued traits in our society. As a parent, it's your place to instill these traits; it's what we call character development. Through years of such training, you have, in effect, taught American deep culture so that your children will grow up to be mature, successful adults.

With your exchange student, you will want to make sure that your rules and procedures are understood and followed, just as they are by everyone else in the household, but your reasons for presenting rules will not be entirely the same. With your exchange student, character development is not your responsibility. With your exchange student, you are one step removed from direct parenting and more like a grandparent, as we explained briefly in chapter 3.

More specifically, what you are is an educator. As such, your role is to teach your student about your household rules and expectations so that he can temporarily adjust to your family's patterns and by so doing, learn about a different way of life. Here's how one host father put it.

> It's our job to tell Caesar about us and how our family works. I try to explain our customs and procedures and why they exist. We make a special point of saying that our guidelines are just that— guidelines, not ultimatums or fixed absolutes or veiled threats.

> Of course, Caesar makes mistakes. When he
> forgets or questions something, it doesn't mean he's
> immature, a bad person, or a potential misfit in
> society. It usually means we need to talk.

Because you will be in a special role as an educator and quasi parent, you will want to approach the topic of rules and expectations with tolerance and sensitivity, while at the same time making sure that important procedures are respected and followed. Juggling all of this is not an easy task. Indeed, finding just the right blend of patience, flexibility, and firmness can be difficult. After all, while you don't want to be harsh about violations, you will need to provide guidance and discipline to your student who is, after all, a minor in your care.

To help you remember the relativity of your household rules and expectations, bear in mind that when your student leaves your home and returns to his own country, he will have to "unlearn" much of what you have taught him about appropriate behavior.[†] If you have taught him that it is wrong to slurp his soup, that he should make his own bed, that he must be home by the eleven o'clock curfew, that it's permissible to joke with his teachers—these may be some of the hundreds of things he has to unlearn when he goes home to his own country and natural family. If he doesn't, he could face criticism from his own parents and friends, as one Brazilian student explains.

> I love my American family, but now I'm going back.
> I'm nervous because I must forget all my American ways. If I make mistakes, my father won't understand why. He won't understand there are different ways. He will say to me, "We sent you to the United States, a better culture, and you came back acting like trash!"

[†] Of course, there will be much that your student will retain and take home with him, learning and experiences that will influence him for years to come: special friendships with you and his classmates, knowledge of cultural differences, new skills, and broadened horizons.

Make Discussions a "Learning Experience"

A little empathy with your student will go a long way. If you were the exchange student, you certainly wouldn't want to receive a series of lectures about what is "right and wrong," so make sure this isn't how you approach the task. As one host father expresses it,

> Household agreements should not be presented as edicts from heaven. Rigid rules only force kids to disobey. They're an invitation for a collision. It's important to present general agreements and then to bend with the situation.
>
> Here's what I mean: we told Siri, "Generally speaking, we want you home by eleven P.M. However, we know there'll be exceptions. If something comes up, talk with us beforehand and we'll reach a compromise."

Also, remember that your student's sense of confidence may be a bit fragile due to the turmoil of facing a major adjustment. This can make it difficult to accept criticism, and he may even become defensive if given harsh instructions.

Approach these discussions as a learning experience for both of you. For example, while explaining one of your family's rules, invite your exchange student to describe how his family handles a comparable situation. In addition, discuss rules in terms of what they reflect about each culture's beliefs and standards. This can help your student gain an understanding that goes beyond lifestyle sharing to the broader dimension of culture learning. It also emphasizes that learning and sharing is a two-way process.

Incidentally, when host families express a genuine interest in other cultures, students are often more comfortable conforming to their hosts' way of life.

Explain Rules Thoroughly

For your own children, family rules are generally so well understood that you need only give brief reminders of what's expected. But a brief reminder isn't enough for an exchange student who comes from a different family with agreements and expectations of its own. Consequently, it is important that you not understate the guidelines that you expect your student to follow.

An example of an understated rule is: "If you're not coming home after school, call." A more specific and exact version is the following:

> If you're not planning to be home from school by four o'clock, call and let us know your plans. A courtesy call is an important procedure in our culture and in our household. As a family, it helps us plan our dinner time and keeps us from worrying about what might have happened to you.
>
> There's more to it too. By the time you're seventeen, your own parents may treat you more as an adult and not expect the same kind of checking in. As American parents, we still view you as a minor and will want to know your whereabouts. It's a cultural thing.

Be Patient: Learning Rules Takes Time

Even though your student will be making a sincere effort to adapt, it is not an easy task, and it takes time. You may have explained very clearly that he is to call and let you know where he is, and he may genuinely mean to do so, but it may still take quite a while before he calls you every time.

It's easy to understand how this can happen, especially if he has never had to do this before. When he's out with his new friends, finding a phone may not take on the urgency that you might hope it would. Or he might suppose that, since he called you yesterday and today he's with the same friends doing the same things, you would assume that everything is fine and a call is unnecessary.

Why does this kind of reaction happen? Your student, like everyone else, uses his judgment to decide how and when to apply the rules you have set. Problems can arise because his judgment is based on his experience back home—in his own culture and with his own parents.

It can take a while before he has enough experience in American culture to interpret your guidelines as if he were an American teenager. Then and only then will he be successful.

Watch for Tension

When spoken rules are broken, it's usually fairly obvious what the problem is. Not so with unspoken rules. When they are breached, we may not be able to say exactly what has happened, but we usually sense that something is wrong. That's because our internal alarms have gone off to alert us that something is not right. Try to watch for the uneasy feeling you get. It's a "red alert" (as described in chapter 6). With practice, you'll then be able to identify the unspoken rule that has been breached and explore the situation with your student. Keep in mind the bridging skills described in chapter 6 and Appendix B.

Don't Apply the "Insult Rule"

One of deep culture's most powerful forces is the "Insult Rule."[‡] It reads like this: If you really want to deliberately offend someone, break a cultural rule. You can deliberately offend by refusing to shake hands, showing up late for a dinner party, standing too close, staring, and so on—and making sure you don't apologize. Or you can inadvertently offend by doing these things without knowing you are breaking a rule—which is what often happens with exchange students.

Being unaware of American cultural patterns, exchange students are frequently breaking our rules, failing to apologize, and unintentionally evoking the Insult Rule, meaning we erroneously assume their offensive behavior is deliberate. As one host father states, "In the hosting situation, 99.99 percent of the time an insult is not an insult. It is a simple mistake. It only becomes an insult if *we* make it one."

[‡] This is a term developed by the authors and comes out of their intercultural research and their work as cross-cultural counselors with teenage exchange students and host families.

Don't Trivialize "Trivial Misunderstandings"

It was just six days before Christmas when Inge, a Danish student, told the sponsoring organization that her host mother had said she could "just pack her things and leave their home." After listening to both sides, the organization's representative still felt somewhat baffled as to why things had gotten so out of hand. He lamented, "It takes so little to make a major misunderstanding."

In many cases, the culprit is deep culture. Underneath the little disagreements and the seemingly insignificant misbehavior are "sacred" cultural rules that have been violated. When this happens, people tend to react quite negatively, although they usually aren't sure exactly why. Furthermore, it is the day-to-day events, the seemingly *minor* incidents that tend to cause the *worst* misunderstandings because it is at those moments that we are hit by culture's absolutes that we never even suspected were there.

To minimize overreactions and ultimatums, try to remember that cultural rules affect every aspect of our daily lives. Trivia is no exception.

Heart-to-Heart Talks

Presenting and discussing your household agreements is necessary and can be quite revealing, but it's also important to open lines of deeper communication. This means engaging in some serious discussions, or heart-to-heart talks, in which thoughts and feelings may be freely shared.

Many families find it awkward to sit down formally for a heart-to-heart talk, though for some families this is a normal pattern. More typical is the spontaneous discussion that might take place during the course of a long drive home, or when you have waited up for your exchange student, and he sits on the stairs with you and tells you all about his evening. Some families find that the dinner table is an ideal setting for these discussions.

Not all students will open up quickly, especially when they are still struggling to express themselves in a new language.

If you find that your times alone with the student feel awkward, or if you haven't felt a sense of developing closeness through this kind of heart-to-heart discussion, try to take more initiative in creating the atmosphere that will lead to the habit of talking often and openly.

Several issues that are important to consider when you engage in discussions with your student follow.

Listen to Your Student

It's sometimes hard to listen. Your brain works much faster than another person can talk, especially if that person is searching for the right words in an unfamiliar language. You may be thinking of the half-dozen things you have to get done before tomorrow's staff meeting while your student is trying to explain why he is confused about something that happened at school. It might seem as if you now have one more unwelcome problem on your plate.

You'll find that you can concentrate better once you stop worrying about solving this new problem of his and focus instead on listening for clues that help you understand how he thinks about the world and what he feels. (There are other skills that promote good communication. See Appendix B for details.)

Voice Your Acceptance

Families sometimes forget to tell exchange students they are indeed wanted and accepted. Or families sometimes express their caring in ways that are misunderstood.

For example, one student began tensing up with stomach cramps before meals because his refusal to sample new foods or take second helpings was misinterpreted by the family as a rejection of their hospitality. If you find yourself tempted to "bake someone happy," explain that Americans often use food to express how much they like another person. Then state verbally (rather than through food) that the student is welcome and wanted.

Describe Your Family in Unexceptional Terms

As a host, remind your student that he has come to live with ordinary folks, whose lives are filled with unexceptional, everyday experiences. Point out what is normal and typical in your day-to-day living and clarify what you anticipate will make the homestay experience special within the context of real-life possibilities. For example, explain that a large part of this experience will consist of sharing pretty average daily events. But it is in sharing ordinary activities that people come to know each other and feel comfortable. With a close relationship can come an exciting exchange of ideas and learning.

Explain What It Means to Participate in Someone's Lifestyle

Explain that although you want your student to try living like an American, you are not asking him to renounce his own culture and in effect become "Americanized." Point out that involvement means (1) experimenting with and sampling U.S. ways of doing things and (2) learning the rules and skills necessary to participate in your family and American culture as fully as possible.

Explain the Meaning of Chores

If you're like many Americans, everyone in the household is expected to help with the upkeep of the home by performing specific chores. Because you want your exchange student to participate fully in your home, you'll want to assign him chores, too. But before you do, you may need to explain the following: (1) it is customary in U.S. families to pitch in and help with the housekeeping rather than employ housekeepers; (2) while your family or others in your neighborhood might actually hire someone to come in and clean periodically, each individual still tidies up after him- or herself and helps with the routine daily chores; and (3) many American parents believe that household responsibilities develop the character traits of responsibility, dependability, and thoroughness.

In other cultures, parents often have totally different ways of fostering maturity, so your student may not approach chores with a great deal of seriousness. With this in mind, you might assign your student some household task to give him the opportunity to experience an American custom rather than for the purpose of developing or testing maturity.

Ask your student to describe his family's procedures for maintaining the home and his parents' methods for fostering his character development. In some cases, students explain that their sojourn is their parents' way of encouraging independent decision making and broadened horizons.

Talk about Possible Feelings of Indebtedness

Occasionally students are uncomfortable knowing that families generally receive no compensation for hosting. Feeling indebted for what is being done on their behalf, some students believe they must repay the family's kindness by never complaining, constantly looking happy, and always putting their hosts' wants before their own. This kind of guilt-motivated "good behavior" can keep a student from being himself and may lead to smoldering resentment.

To counter this tendency, make it clear to your student that he is welcome to express his opinions freely, to have his own likes and dislikes, to say no when he needs to, and to make mistakes. (Some other topics you may wish to review and discuss are found in Appendix A.)

Lest you fear that you'll never be able to remember everything we've described in this chapter, take a deep breath and relax. While there may be moments that try your patience, you won't encounter all the issues or all the situations that we've presented. No family does. In the end, when you've given it your best, we hope you'll be rewarded with an affectionate farewell note similar to the one which a departing student left for her family.

> There were some ups and downs, but we managed to solve all the problems [and] I really appreciate all the things you and your family did for me. I love you, but I can't find the words to say it. Maybe someday I will have the words to describe my feelings. A big part of me will remain here. I will love you always.

$$-13-$$

Stage Four: Culture Shock

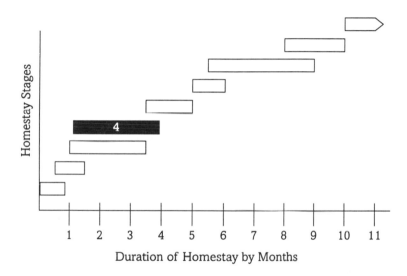

Duration of Homestay by Months

The culture shock stage begins roughly at the end of the first month and extends until the fourth month. Generally, it covers a three-month period. This stage somewhat overlaps in time with the previous stage.*

---

* For some, culture shock may appear at a somewhat later period. Also, some will deny that it affects them no matter how apparent or severe the symptoms. Finally, a few students seem to breeze through without suffering from culture shock at all, although this might be attributable either to their skill in hiding symptoms or to the failure of others to perceive them. The information in this chapter, therefore, should be applied and adapted to fit your particular student.

As students and hosts get to know each other, as the household rules are clarified, and as discussions become deeper and more substantive, exchange students begin to feel involved. At the same time, learning about another way of life makes it clear that there are innumerable confusing differences. Culture shock and a lot of noisy clashing can be the consequence, often expressed as

- dread about going to school because everyone is "arrogant," "superficial," or "stupid," and American high schools are "disgusting,"
- lashing out in anger because of an innocent remark at the dinner table, or retreating teary-eyed to a bedroom,
- longing for family and friends back home who "really understand,"
- ignoring rules or exhibiting unusual shyness, or
- escalating minor squabbles with other family members into standoffs.

At times, the threats to deep culture are quite direct. This was the experience of Leena, a Finnish student, who became anxious each Sunday morning. Church attendance was central to her hosts' way of life but very foreign to Leena; for her, participating in church services caused a conflict, an internal battle between her hosts' beliefs and her own cherished values.

> I would go to the parish with my family because this was a big part of their life. But I felt very funny dressing up and going to church. I would sit there singing songs that meant nothing to me and saying amen to statements I didn't believe in. I felt like a hypocrite who was living one big lie. Each Sunday I would sit there wondering, "Who am I, and what am I doing here?"

Trying to comfort a student going through such agonizing moments of self-doubt can be difficult. Furthermore, because hosts want their student to have pleasant experiences, they sometimes try to cajole their student or pretend that culture shock does not exist. Here is how a host mother describes her disbelief.

When Juanita, our first exchange student, locked herself in her bedroom and cried all afternoon, wanted to sleep with the light on, and complained that our food tasted like sawdust, I concluded that I wasn't being a good host.

After all, houseguests never cry or want to go home unless you treat them bad, right? So, I set out on this big campaign to pull her out of it. "Let's shower this kid with love and really get her involved," I told my husband. When that didn't work, I started scolding her: "If you really wanted to, you could feel good." You see, I was convinced Juanita was just being stubborn or disobedient or lazy. Culture shock? That's a bunch of bunk! I believed that if she really wanted to, Juanita could feel great, get involved at school, and make lots of friends.

And when that also failed to happen, I called the sponsoring organization and complained to them, saying they'd made a bad choice with Juanita. "You didn't prepare her for this experience," I informed them. Through all of this, I just couldn't accept the reality of what culture shock does to a person.

For this host mother, several exchange students had come and gone before she developed an in-depth appreciation of the impact of culture. For her, the change was a gradual process that entailed going through a series of learning steps and developing new strengths and skills. Specifically, this involved (1) recognizing her own feelings of disbelief, (2) developing a tolerance for the strong feelings experienced by her students, (3) noticing that most of her students went through similar unsettling experiences and concluding that culture shock reactions must be a normal part of living in a new culture, (4) realizing that in time, culture shock runs its course and the symptoms begin to fade, and (5) developing practical techniques for being of assistance. Commenting on her own learning, this same host mother said,

Now that I can tolerate culture shock in our exchange students, I'm freed up from being the res-

cuer. Now I can empathize, give support, and be of
real help.

As a cultural adviser, there is something more you need to
keep in mind: the unsettling experiences of culture shock can
become important learning opportunities, so you don't want
to rob your student of something with such potential benefit.
When Leena asked herself, "Who am I? What am I doing
here?" she was grappling with questions that were fundamental
to her own personal development. If she had not been exposed to the religious life of her host family, it could have
been many years before she started to pose these questions
to herself about her own beliefs and spiritual values. Much of
the educational value of the exchange experience comes when
students can address these questions and meet these life challenges with insight and personally satisfying solutions.

Of course, it is rarely easy to go through such intensive
learning or, for that matter, to watch someone struggling with
the issues of identity and values. So bear in mind that your
own discomfort is part of the overall process, just as it was
when you watched your baby's teething or worried about that
first day of school, the arrival of puberty, and so on. Now
your student is going through an experience of similar mag-
nitude, and her reactions to cultural changes are what we
describe as culture shock.

Ways You Can Help
Ease Your Student's Distress

Discuss Culture Shock Behavior

When your student feels comfortable talking, discuss the
causes of culture shock, point out the ways that students typically experience it,[†] and explain that culture shock is part of a
very intense learning process that can have lifelong benefits.
Such explanations can help her accept it as normal and tem-

---

† For details, see the review of symptoms in chapter 7.

porary. This is important because sometimes students mistakenly believe that culture shock only happens to those who are "weak-willed," "immature," or "poorly adjusted."

What else can you say or do to be helpful? One host mother says the following to her students: "I understand there will be times when you feel bad. It's okay. Sometimes talking about it helps the discomfort go away. So if you want to talk, I'm available." Another helpful message is this: "Culture shock is normal. If I were in your country, I'd be feeling just like you are."

Encourage "Reaching-Out" Behavior

It's important that a student find ways of reaching out to others. Help your student share her feelings, but keep in mind that it is not always easy to talk about personal matters. At first your student might only open up with you or with one of your children. It is also common for exchange students to look for friends and confidantes among other exchange students who are also going through similar experiences.

As your student experiences success with these initial efforts, she should be encouraged to find additional ways of reaching out. She might get involved in some school activity, or go to a movie with a neighbor, and so forth. In each instance, encourage her to move at a pace and in a direction that suits her needs and personality and that she can handle successfully. If your student seems to feel most comfortable around your family, think about inviting a family with teenagers or another host family and their student to join you for a potluck dinner, for pizza out, for bowling, or for an evening of home videos.

Allow for "Time-Out" Periods

Culture shock reactions are rarely continuous; typically, they come and go. One day a student will be fine, the next day she may feel miserable. When you sense that she is having a difficult time, refrain from deep or complicated discussions, avoid teaching new customs or new household routines, and minimize additional stress. Think of these as "coasting" or "time-out" periods, when communication and learning are postponed.

Time-outs are important because culture shock is an anxiety reaction to change, and people do not function well or think clearly when they are anxious. They tend, instead, to be argumentative and defensive, and if pressured, they can become defiant and panic-stricken.

When Leena could not cope because of culture shock, her host family suggested that she stay home on Sundays, knowing that church services made her uneasy. Given this time-out, Leena's nervousness began to subside. Later, feeling more secure, she began to attend church services occasionally by her own choice.

Expect Periodic Withdrawal

There are times when a student just does not want to be involved in much of anything and might withdraw temporarily. This may occur because she is feeling confused, mentally exhausted, or homesick. Needing time to be alone, rest, and think things through, she may retreat to her bedroom and close the door. As one student stated, "In those moments I just needed my 'lonely time.'"

If, during these withdrawal periods, your student seems to be oblivious to your existence, try not to view this behavior as a sign of rejection. One host mother explained the situation well when she said, "It's not that your student doesn't love you; it's that during this ordeal of culture shock, sometimes she simply can't."

This does not mean that you should encourage your student to stay alone in her room for days on end—even if that is what she seems to want to do. Students who withdraw too much are not helped by excessive isolation, so do not ignore the distress calls of a student who avoids all contact with family members or who shuts herself in her room every evening. Such a student might feel that she is unable to adjust to your family's lifestyle, and she may be afraid to say what's bothering her.

Through difficult times, your best course is to invite and encourage discussion, find ways to show her your interest and acceptance, and bring up your concerns with the exchange organization or with attentive teachers who may be able to help.[‡]

Expect Disagreements and Respond to Them

If disagreements develop between your student and your children, try to minimize the amount of time they spend together. Then explain to your children that your exchange student may not have the energy, at present, to be a friend.

Be Prepared for Judgmental Remarks

At some point you will hear your student reacting to your ways of doing things with red alert comments like "That's stupid" or "How disgusting." As you know, these reactions suggest that your student is struggling with disturbing cultural differences. Keep in mind that this is a reaction to deep culture violations and the unspoken message is "I can't cope." When you hear these remarks, it's a signal to postpone discussions, since your student will probably not be open to your ideas. Instead, try to be empathic and respond by saying something like, "It sounds like our ways don't make any sense to you" or "I can see you are really disgusted and upset about this" or "I'm sorry that you feel this way." At a later time, discuss these red alert reactions in order to promote eye-opener experiences.

Encourage Extra Rest

When things seem bewildering or threatening, as with Leena, students feel physically drained and need extra rest. One host parent explained that for several weeks her student came home from school, ate a small snack, then slept until dinnertime. "Jean-Jacques wasn't being lazy," she explained. "He needed the sleep to recuperate from the 'American high school maze.'"

[‡] Information regarding prolonged and extreme culture shock reactions is provided in chapter 15: "Taking Stock."

Don't Create "No-Exit" Situations

One of the most tempting, and also one of the least helpful, responses any parent can make to a difficult situation is to issue an ultimatum. For example, some students respond to having a hard time by seeking comfort in endless telephone calls to their parents or another exchange student, thus tying up your phone and getting on your nerves.

Although you may have to grit your teeth to keep an ultimatum from popping out, do it. The "No more phone calls, period!" route can create "no-exit" feelings of entrapment and panic, since your student may perceive the telephone calls as a vital lifeline. Such a decree can also seriously undermine rapport and trust, prompting your student to maintain the prohibited phone contact through secretive and devious means. To avoid all this, discuss the matter openly with the student so that underlying issues can be clarified and changes gradually implemented.

Tolerate Your Student's Intense Feelings

Ironically, after a phone call home or a chat with another exchange student, your student may *seem* more agitated than relieved. This frequently occurs because contact with loved ones and conationals can stir up a variety of strong feelings: tenderness, loss, closeness, and relief—all of which may be expressed in an outpouring of tears. However, such moments can be quite beneficial, easing recovery. As one student stated, "I would have feelings jailed up inside of me. I had to liberate them. Crying was the best way. Afterwards, I got better."

Minimize Complications

Just coping with simple things like getting up in the morning, being civil with the family, or concentrating on homework assignments can require a lot of energy and seem like major accomplishments. Because your student may already be coping at maximum effort, try not to create additional stress, such as (1) leaving the student alone for extended periods of time, (2) taking her on trips or to parties, (3) pressuring her to get high grades at school, (4) prohibiting her from calling home or talking to other exchange students, (5) expecting a quick recovery from culture shock, (6) teasing or joking about her "strange" culture shock behavior, or (7) asking her to give talks or show slides of her country to large groups.

In closing, something we said earlier in this chapter bears repeating. It may not be easy for you to see your student struggling with culture shock, even though you are aware of the long-term benefits. Bear in mind that your own discomfort is part of the overall process. Growth from cultural learning may be painful at times but also very rewarding for both of you.

—14—

Stage Five: The Holidays

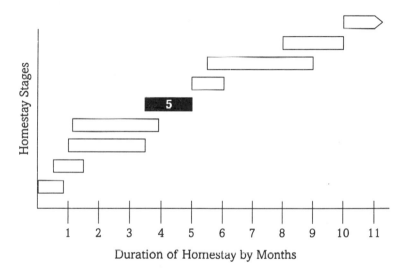

For many American families, the period between Thanksgiving and New Year's is a time of festivities. In both Jewish and Christian households, there is worship and celebration, special foods are prepared, religious vows are renewed, and annual visits from relatives are eagerly anticipated.

Knowing that the holiday season is a time of happiness with loved ones, host families often want to involve their students in their cherished customs and share with them a lively holiday spirit. "We told Marcos that he'd find our Christmas season simply enchanting, and he did," enthused one host mother. "The day we took him caroling, he radiated like a neon sign."

In many cases, expectations for a cheery Christmas are totally fulfilled, but there are also times when the holidays turn out to be more stressful than joyous. Some students are unable to take part in their family's celebrations because they have slipped into a variation of culture shock which we call "the holiday blues."

Why does this happen? With all of the talk about the magic of the holidays, students become preoccupied with memories of loved ones back home. Because their thoughts are elsewhere and because host family traditions may not be familiar, it's possible for a student to begin feeling like an outsider. Then, particularly in the northern states, with winter days turning everything cold and gray like their chilled inner spirit, some students withdraw rather than involve themselves in light-hearted merriment or unfamiliar social situations.

The holiday blues affect about one of every two students and typically result in a period of mild homesickness. For many, the need to call home or retreat for a brief "lonely" time is the only indication that the holidays have been diffi-cult. For others the blues are more severe. One Norwegian girl was so adversely affected that she felt intimidated by the thought of giving gifts or meeting her hosts' relatives. During Christmas week, while her host family was humming carols and hoping for snow, Kari disappeared from sight. She re-treated to her room, got in bed, and bundled up in a huge protective mound of fluffy, warm blankets. There she remained for two days.

If the home Kari was in had been yours, you might have been quite surprised when she said she found it frightening to think about giving presents and visiting relatives. After all, aren't gift giving and socializing enjoyed by everybody? "Good grief," you might have thought, "it never dawned on me that someone could experience our Christmas season as frighten-ing." Next, you might correctly have concluded that Kari's strange behavior was an overreaction—a result of culture shock jitters. When she retreated to her bedroom, you might have responded by looking for ways you could help ease her distress.

Unfortunately, that's not what happened. Kari's host family didn't realize that her behavior was related to holiday blues. Instead, her withdrawal was misinterpreted as rejection. Confused and feeling unwanted, the family failed to perceive Kari's real needs. Here's what the host mother said.

> When Kari retreated to her bedroom, something snapped inside of me. I sort of stepped sideways into a whole different way of behaving. It just happened to me like taking on a stage role. Feelings started boiling up, but I wasn't attuned to them. I reacted on reflex—dashing about being grouchy, feeling put upon and unloved. For two days I kept thinking, "What's wrong with that dumb kid? She's stomping on us! She's messing up our Christmas."
>
> Not once did I stop and think, "Hey, I've lost my objectivity. I need to get back to realistic thoughts and feelings." I had fallen into a different way of functioning and was taking everything personally.

By Christmas Eve this host mother began to see things a bit more clearly. She was still upset, but she did recognize that a communication breakdown existed and outside help was needed.

> Slowly I began to realize that Kari wasn't being mean or punishing; she was frightened and coping the only way she knew how. But still, I felt shut out. My feelings of rejection had gotten so high I just couldn't climb over them and be of help.
>
> So on Christmas Eve, I called a friend who agreed to be our moderator. Ana could see both sides. She helped Kari rejoin the family, and she helped me regain my objectivity.

What Kari and her host family had experienced was a breakdown in communication. The student had slipped into the holiday blues, and the family "stepped a little sideways," going through a brief period of distorted thinking and overreactions. Although collisions like this don't occur with great frequency, even experienced host families report that they periodically face similar dilemmas.

Because you may find yourself at a collision point—either during the holiday season or at some other time during the homestay—the following recommendations are provided.

Plan Ahead

Help your student be a part of your own festivities as well as his natural family's celebration. You might (1) help see that cards and packages are mailed early so that they will reach home in time for the holidays, (2) ask the student to prepare a favorite food or tell you about a custom from home that can be part of your activities here, and (3) help find a good time for him to call home when international circuits aren't too busy.

Keep Your Plans Simple

Sometimes hosts put so much effort into trying to create a perfect holiday season that they also create unnecessary extra pressure for themselves. One family might think that this year they will go out to the countryside to select and cut their own tree just as a special treat for their exchange student, though it means a two-hour drive each way. Another might decide that this would be the year to let the family teenagers have an elaborate New Year's Eve party, splurging a little to hire a DJ for the event. One family may want to make some special efforts to attend tree-lighting ceremonies and caroling parties, or to make sure that everyone comes home for each night of the lighting of the Chanukah candles.

While any and all of these activities are fine and can be fun, they are often time-consuming and can leave you frazzled. It might be better to simply stick to the basics, watch your budget, and take whatever shortcuts you can to make your life less pressured. Enjoy the holiday spirit without the demand that your student must experience the perfect celebration.

Seek Help If Serious Difficulties Arise

If you begin to sense that you are in the midst of a communication impasse, consider bringing in a moderator to help restore understanding, as Kari's family did. Be sure to choose someone who can be impartial and hear both sides clearly. People to consider might be a school counselor, a minister or pastoral counselor, a cross-cultural counselor, a teacher, or any professional who will not take sides.

—15—

Stage Six: Taking Stock

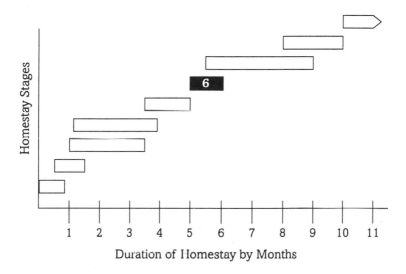

Homestay Stages

6

Duration of Homestay by Months

Stage Six* begins after the holidays and extends for approximately one month.

---

* A new stage, "Taking Stock," has been added to the original eight-stage model developed by the authors. It is the result of recommendations from host families and experts in the field, coupled with an assessment of need by the authors. Previously, some of the material in this chapter was embedded in the culture learning stage in which the reader was alerted to the possibility of lingering adjustment difficulties. The need for families to take stock prior to culture learning was implied. Now that need is addressed directly and with pertinent guidance.

For most of us, January is life's hangover month. We are done in, and it is not just from too much celebrating. More precisely it is the fallout from all that has been ignored during the frenzied holiday season. For much of November and December, Americans tend to take a wide detour from the straight and narrow. We ignore our diets, get too busy to work out at the gym, put off getting the oil changed, and let the bills and catalogues gather dust as we rush off to the mall. Come January, we wake up and find ourselves waist deep in the "never mind syndrome."

It doesn't feel good. Usually, the only solution is to take care of the zillion and one things that have been neglected and get back on track. One area needing attention might be the relationship with your exchange student. If there have been some disagreements or dissatisfactions, chances are they were overlooked during the holidays with dismissives like "It's not that big a deal" or "For now, I'll just ignore that comment."

But we all know that out of sight is not really out of mind, and minor irritations have a way of festering and growing into big problems. You see, there is a tendency to slide from the "never mind" attitude into the "grin and bear it" mode and then wind up in the "Big D"—and, sadly, we don't mean Dallas; there could be a *disaster* in the making.

We doubt that you want to travel down this path. So to make sure your relationship with your exchange student is still a healthy one, some review and evaluation may be called for.[†] Basically, there are several areas that probably deserve your attention as you take stock of where you have been, where you are, and where you are going.

Are You Being Fooled by Boredom?

Boredom should not be confused with a general sense of well-being and contentment or simple inactivity. In most cases,

---

[†] Some sponsoring organizations are beginning to offer midcycle orientations in order to address many of the same issues raised in this chapter. Such programs can be most useful to families, and we recommend them.

boredom is a deficit state, a masked or passive restlessness, or possibly mild depression. Many authorities view boredom as the tip of the iceberg. Just under the surface there is, with fair frequency, irritation, disappointment, or anxiety. Signs of boredom should alert you that problems are brewing—cross-cultural or otherwise.

For example, if your student is complaining that there is nothing to do, that she is bored, the culprit may be the fact that the general activity level in your home is different from what she has been accustomed to. Remember, we discussed these kinds of differences in chapter 7. Now might be a good time to go back and review these differences, discuss them with your student, and devise solutions if appropriate.[‡]

Are You Having Second Thoughts?

When the doubts begin to creep in, and it is almost inevitable that at some point they will, students and families go through a period of soul-searching. Students begin to ask themselves, "Did I make the right decision coming here? Maybe I'd be happier if I'd gone on to college instead of taking the year off for this experience." And hosts can entertain equally mixed feelings, such as "This is costing us a lot of money. Is it really worth it?"

The best solution is usually to go back and re-examine the expectations that you identified in chapter 11. Were they, in fact, realistic? And if so, are they being met? If not, maybe the problem is that you and your student are, in some ways, still back in one of the earlier stages—such as stage three (Deepening the Relationship) or four (Culture Shock).

Are You Stuck in a Rut?

If you are not progressing through the stages, you might feel disappointment and frustration, and the hosting experience could turn sour. Signs of being stuck are described next.

[‡] Other reasons for discomfort with the activity level might be changes due to the constraints of winter or a contrast between holiday and nonholiday schedules. In any regard, discussion is probably warranted.

Deep Culture Noise. If you are hearing a lot of static in your communications, the culprit could be deep culture noise. Make sure you are taking the time to explain family rules—both the obvious and not so obvious ones. Also, make sure you are using the bridging skills outlined in Appendix B. Doing so should help minimize deep culture noise.

Prolonged and Severe Culture Shock Reactions. In chapter 13, the normal culture shock reactions were presented. These include minor changes in appetite, moodiness and mild depression, increased smoking, disturbance of sleep patterns, occasional irritability or withdrawal, faultfinding or exaggerated praise of the host culture, and homesickness. Only rarely do students experience extreme reactions over a prolonged period of time or become unusually disruptive. If you are noticing such a pattern, professional help may be called for.

What is an extreme reaction? There are several types of behavior that should be taken seriously and signal a need for outside help: (1) several days of excessive sleeping or insomnia, (2) eating patterns leading to a significant weight gain or loss, (3) prolonged acute depression, (4) illegal behavior such as shoplifting or vandalism, (5) repeated use of illicit drugs or heavy alcohol consumption, (6) drastic decline in school grades or truancy, (7) serious communication barriers with the host family, and (8) thoughts of suicide and preoccupation with morbid topics.

If your student experiences one or more of the above reactions, it may be an indication of a very intense—though still normal—culture shock reaction, which will subside with time if special support is provided. On the other hand, there are times when what appears to be an intense culture shock reaction may be a symptom of more fundamental problems. Sorting out the difference and recommending appropriate interventions should be left to professionals.

If you desire more specific information about any of these behaviors or if you have concerns that your student's culture shock reactions may be extreme in nature, we suggest you seek consultation. The sponsoring organization's local representative is the first person to contact, and he or she should be able to put you in touch with professionals who have cross-cultural counseling expertise and can make professional assessments.

Broken-Record Remarks. Back in the good ole days of LP records, a bad scratch on a favorite song would catch the needle in a groove, causing the same phrase to play over and over again. At times, exchange students can sound like broken records when they repeat the same complaints day in and day out. Such remarks are a tip-off about some inner discomfort. Some families hear broken-record remarks each evening during the local TV news. When crime reports are aired, students may be prone to announce, "We don't have these problems in my country." Ignoring the comments doesn't help. Neither does the retort, "We already know that, Miguel." A better way to handle broken-record remarks is to turn them into eye-openers; if your student is constantly commenting on crime reports, for example, perhaps she is fearful of becoming a victim of crime, and these concerns need to be acknowledged and dealt with realistically.

Preoccupation with the Future. Adolescence is a time of looking ahead, of challenges such as choosing a college, selecting a career, finding a mate, and moving out on one's own. This is normal, and discussions about future plans can be quite productive. But an unhealthy preoccupation with these matters can suggest that more immediate concerns are being avoided. It can be much easier to fantasize about the future than to focus on thorny adjustment problems in the present. You will want to make sure this is not happening with your student.

Too Many Calls Home. If by this time telephone calls home exceed two or more a month (not including birthdays, holidays, or emergencies), it may be an indication that your student is encountering adjustment difficulties.[1] We don't recommend that you or anyone else abruptly stop the calls, since they may be an important lifeline. Instead, discuss the matter with your student and with the sponsoring organization's representative. Remember, it is not the phone calls per se that are the problem; the excessive calls may be a signal that there are adjustment difficulties and help is needed.

"No-Naming." Remember our earlier discussion about settling on the names you and your student use to address each other? Now might be a good time to double-check that you have not resorted to something called "no-naming." That is what happens when, instead of having satisfactory, comfortable ways of addressing each other, the student or the family goes through all kinds of contortions to avoid using names to get the other's attention.

Consider this for a moment: are you beginning to wonder if your student thinks of you as "'Scuse Me," as in "'Scuse Me, would you pass the remote?" or do you now have names that are used with relative ease? If not, or if in doubt, we suggest you talk it over. This, incidentally, is another situation where you can begin by clarifying whether any cross-cultural differences are involved. For example, ask the student to explain how she addresses her parents at home and how that might differ from the way your children address you. Discuss any differences that you uncover, and use this information to guide you. Make sure that you both arrive at names you can use with ease, especially if nicknames are involved.

Friendlessness. Not having an American friend can be most distressing to a teenage exchange student, perhaps less so for boys whose friends tend to be more casual and activity-oriented, and more so for girls who may be accustomed to having close confidantes. If this is the plight of your student, a discussion of the following may be in order.

Although most foreigners do not expect friendship to just happen—like love at first sight—they often expect it to happen fairly easily. But making friends is an elaborate ritual, like a dance with numerous defined moves and countermoves. The process seems nonexistent to insiders because it is part of their deep culture. But exchange students can experience a chilling awkwardness when they try to "break the ice" and get acquainted or, worse yet, deepen the relationship to that of close friends. Most just do not know the rules for doing it right or doing it smoothly.

A second reason for frustration can be this: in the United States people seek out friends with whom they share hobbies and mutual interests. But in many other cultures, friendships are family-based so that children grow up with a ready-made set of friends from among their familiy's circle of relatives and social ties. Exchange students from the latter group often erroneously conclude that American friends will be provided for them by their host brother or sister's circle of friends. Not knowing how to take the initiative and seek out friends can be disconcerting and annoying.

If your student is finding it especially difficult to make friends with American teens, one solution may be to teach her to use what one organization calls the "Your Ticket In" strategy.§ To do this, help your student identify personal qualities or talents that others would find appealing and suggest ways that these assets can be promoted to build friendships. Incidentally, it is not unusual for exchange students to say their best friends are other exchange students with whom they share the "hard times" of adjustment. Americans tend to remain as acquaintances—somewhat superficial relationships and perhaps even a bit strained. Certainly, in any culture, deep, intimate friendships can take more than a few months to blossom.

---

§ In their orientations, Youth for Understanding trainers encourage exchange students to use this strategy, and they rehearse it in role-playing situations.

Endnotes

[1] Cornelius Grove, *Orientation Handbook for Youth Exchange Programs* (Yarmouth, ME: Intercultural Press, 1989), 36.

—16—

Stage Seven: Culture Learning

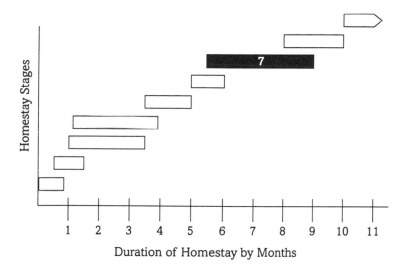

Duration of Homestay by Months

Stage Seven begins in the fifth month and extends through the eighth. Typically it covers a four-month period.

In the fifth or sixth month, a delightful chain reaction can be set in motion for hosts and their students. It often begins once students have settled back into normal routines after the holiday excitement. Feeling more inwardly secure, they typically experience a marked improvement in their language skills, which in turn increases their capacity to share their feelings and thoughts. They come alive, radiating both depth and vitality, and begin to be seen by the family as more interesting,

more three-dimensional, more understandable, and more re-
sponsive as "friends."

For many, this is a time when an overall comfortable fit
shows up in easy-flowing but serious talks, laughter, and moments of comfortable silence. "It's just good rapport," remarks
one host mother.

> Like tapping the beat to your favorite song, you
> feel in sync. Your student fires off, "Guess what?!"
> and you come in right on cue. There's a private
> language of inside jokes, slangy expressions, and
> goofy smirks. You sit and talk about nothing for
> hours, and you can telegraph knowing glances with
> a raise of the brow or dance of the eyes. Every-
> thing comes smooth and easy except, of course,
> when you deliberately spark little spats to tease and
> get under the skin—just the slightest little bit.

As March rolls around, you may become acutely aware of
how fast time is passing and experience a desire to deepen
the relationship as much as possible. A turning point is reached,
and there is an urgency to take advantage of all that can be
learned and enjoyed.

> It hits you that the experience is half over; in a few
> short months a plane will be lifting off with your
> exchange student on it!
> Suddenly, there's hardly any time left, and
> there's so much you want to learn about this per-
> son. So with the clock ticking, you begin to make
> every minute count.

To make this stage special, outings to historical sites might be
planned, frequent trips made to the library to explore aspects
of the student's culture, or Saturdays spent in the kitchen learning how to cook the student's favorite dishes. At times, the
dinner hour may extend late into the evening because your
student has developed a knack for sparking lively discussions
about cultural differences, American lifestyles, or some con-
troversial topic. For some students and families, this phase of
the homestay is a time of serious introspection, growing pains,
and heightened cultural self-awareness.

It is also not uncommon during this stage for students to seek their hosts' opinions and recommendations about matters that pertain to life back home. Confidential talks can develop about such things as mixed feelings for a girl- or boyfriend, disagreements with natural parents, doubts about one's identity and values, or uncertainties regarding a career direction. In these discussions, the host (who serves as an adult friend to the student) can provide unique help, which is not usually available from the adolescent's peers. And in the process, something grows out of the experience. As one mother notes,

> Whenever you work together to reach a new understanding about some cultural difference, a mispronounced word, some confusing behavior, or a shocking new experience, you'll feel a sense of accomplishment. This is not accomplishment for having solved a particular problem, but accomplishment in terms of helping the relationship go one step deeper.
>
> When I notice us moving in closer on the couch, when we can laugh about crazy situations, when we become comfortable with silent moments—all these things tell me the relationship is going well, and it really feels right. All at once I think, "Oh, boy! This exchange student is really somebody who belongs in my life."

Occasionally, the bonds between hosts and students become so special, so deep, that they could be considered *confianzas*, the Spanish word for unusually meaningful, caring friendships. One mother who has hosted numerous students explains that for her family, a few students were really "super special." Although hard to define exactly, her confianzas all had this in common: there was a right chemistry, a sharing of important values, and having the sense of "making a positive difference in this kid's life."

The Inward Journey

This is going to sound surprising, but just experiencing another culture rarely changes attitudes and perceptions. In fact, negative stereotypes can become even more strongly entrenched at times. In my own experience, living in an African country for three and a half years did not help dissipate certain cultural stereotypes I had about the people there. Bribery seemed to be rampant. It disturbed me because I could not deal with it. And I became very negative when confronted by it on numerous occasions. To me it was very wrong, quite a culture shock.

Some years later when my experiences in that culture were behind me, I began a second journey—an inner spiritual one—as I began thinking deeply about cross-cultural issues. From having a narrow mindset and believing that some cultures were less civilized, I began to understand that *difference* was not *deficit,* and that no one has the right to judge another culture by one's own values. I realized that I had no right to judge Africans by my value system simply because they didn't behave in the "accepted ways." It was awesome coming to such a realization. But it has been liberating.[1]

These insightful words are from a woman who teaches a class in cross-cultural psychology at Northern Territory University in Darwin, Australia. A native of Sri Lanka, she explains to her students that neither overseas experience nor classroom education necessarily removes the cultural blind spots one might have. To do so requires a conscious effort to learn about culture, to learn about the influences that it has on one's own behavior, and to learn tolerance for different value systems and different ways of behaving. All this must occur, she explains, if we are to learn to appreciate and value people who are not like us.

That's what the second, inner journey is all about: the nonjudgmental acceptance of different values and different behaviors. It is also what we hope this chapter will help you discover: how to better appreciate cultural differences by taking this kind of journey yourself.

One host mother's inward journey began with late-night

talks with her student, between 11:00 P.M. and 3:00 A.M. "That's when it was quiet, everyone's guard was down, and we could talk freely," she confides. One such evening, her German student wandered in and began talking about his life at home. The mother describes what happened.

> I was curious to learn about Ulrich's family background, but when he told me he had no curfew at home and frequently rode the train alone across Europe, I didn't believe him. I thought, "He's just trying to persuade me to let up on our rules." Then I thought, "Maybe he has that freedom in Germany, but it's certainly a sign that his parents are weird." My next thought was, "Ulrich's freedom is probably very limited. He probably has no curfews on weekends and can ride only certain safe trains."

You might notice a parallel between this mother's experience and that of Axel, the German boy described in chapter 4. You'll recall that Axel couldn't believe that in the United States boys as a rule are not allowed to visit girls in their bedrooms. Before he could accept this difference between the two cultures, Axel went through a series of reactions very similar to that of Ulrich's host mother. Initially, she denied what she had heard, thought her exchange student was trying to manipulate her, surmised that his parents were "weird," and concluded that he was only telling her half-truths.

But the mother decided to delve deeper. She recognized that, at one level, she held some ideas about unsupervised travel and curfews—ideas coming from her own deep culture—that differed from the rules which were enforced by her student's parents in Germany. At the cultural level, she and her student were talking about behaviors and attitudes that were different because they were based on two distinct approaches to life. Here is more of what the mother thought to herself.

> It's my belief that teenagers need to be in bed early on weeknights so they'll be rested for school. This means that we as parents have to set a curfew for them.

Ulrich has just told me his German parents know that he will want to get adequate rest and will therefore get to bed at a reasonable time without a curfew. If he'd told me this three months ago, I wouldn't have believed him. But now I trust him and respect what he says. You know, I'm beginning to realize that there's a big difference in our two families' definitions of responsibility. We Americans put responsibility in the parents' hands; German parents give more responsibility to their children.

Another reason I set a curfew for our kids seems to stem from my belief that teenagers who stay out late are up to no good; the boys are raising hell, and the girls are getting into trouble. In the U.S. kids are taught that wholesome weekend socializing ends about midnight.

But Ulrich has pointed out that in Germany, it is customary on weekends for teenagers to be out after midnight sitting in cafes drinking beer, dancing, and talking philosophy. It seems that teenagers socialize at different times and in different ways in the two cultures.

Regarding travel, I would never permit our teenage son to ride a train alone across the U.S. I don't think it's safe. Besides, it's just not done here.

Now I understand that trains in Europe are sleek and safe. Everyone rides them. My student says that asking a German to avoid trains would be like asking an American to stay away from cars and freeways. Besides, he says Germans believe in "wanderlust"; they believe that travel is important—it has the power to educate young minds.

After exploring these issues, both the student and the host mother had a better understanding of why teenagers are supervised differently in the two cultures. Of course, the mother still expected Ulrich to follow the rules for teenagers in her household, but she had a new appreciation for cultural differences and why her student could not automatically fit into her family's way of functioning. She could also better understand why long, serious discussions are necessary to develop an appreciation for another's way of life. What's more, the host mother began to recognize some of her cultural blind spots and cultural innocence, as she states about their session in intercultural learning:

> I realized I wasn't initially able to believe Ulrich because I'd been looking at German behavior with American eyes; I was trapped in my Americanization. To understand Ulrich, I had to see things through his eyes. When I made that shift, I realized, "Gee, it really is very different somewhere else!"

What this mother was eventually able to do illustrates what cultural learning is all about: being able to accept your own biases, then suspending them in order to take up residence in another person's point of view. During the culture learning stage, biases and disbelief generally give way to respect, deeper understanding, and the capacity to be able to say:

> I can understand why you think and feel the way you do. In your country, your behavior and customs are just as logical and appropriate as mine. As they say in Brazil, "*O que é diferente não é obrigatoriamente errado*"—What is different is not necessarily wrong.

It has now been many years since we first talked with one of the host mothers who helped develop some of this chapter's ideas about culture learning. Many of her former exchange students, she muses, are now married with children of their own.

> I'm a host grandmother, and my own thirteen-year-old granddaughter has exchange cousins. We're many generations now. My husband and I have stopped counting how many students we've hosted over the years. It's close to twenty or more, I'm sure. This year we've got a six-foot-eight, eighteen year-old from the Netherlands. And he's terrific!
>
> For us, hosting is in some ways like a marriage—learning to live with someone and the surprises that spring out of the box. Some days I learn

something about Joost and his preferences. Some days I learn something about myself when I encounter his perception of me. At other times, I find myself looking at him, and he's looking back at me because we're making different assumptions about the same experience. That used to be upsetting to me. Now it's fascinating.

Two decades of hosting have given this host family some marvelous memories. The experiences have also changed them in innumerable ways, making them more open-minded, more appreciative of diversity, and less rigid and enthnocentric. "Each new student stretches us in some way," she explains. "There are always new ideas, new experiences, new visions of what might be—it's all made us quite elastic."

The experience of hosting has also had a ripple effect, influencing this host mother's daily life in subtle but pervasive ways chiefly unrelated to hosting. In everyday conversations, empathy and sensitivity punctuate her engaging communication style, a pleasing manner which noticeably takes into account both her own and others' interests. For her, this approach to relationships just comes naturally now. "The dual perspective isn't something I have to go looking for," she explains with modest pride. "It just pops up unexpectedly."

Equally important, there is ample evidence that over the years, this mother has honed the skills of critical thinking and learned alternatives to Western linear-thinking patterns[2] by considering rival, competing ideas. And, she has learned to closely analyze information for its accuracy and underlying assumptions. She related the following experience as an example.

Recently I attended a lecture by a dignitary from Australia who implied that the Aborigines were uneducable, subhuman. He seemed blinded to the reality that there could be things more important to these people than Western values—like learning how to read and write in English. As a prisoner in darkness, he couldn't see beyond his own assumptions.

As he went on and on, I realized, "This person in high office is extremely biased and doesn't even know it." I felt embarrassed, like standing up and shouting, "Mr. Distinguished Speaker, stop and think about what you are saying. These are real people!"

I was just shocked to hear things that sounded so skewed. I expected that someone in his position would either have shed such beliefs or learned to not dare speak them publicly. I wondered if others in the audience were reaching the same conclusions, and I was glad I have learned how to size up situations for myself.

What's ahead for families like hers who seem to have experienced so much and taken cross-cultural encounters to the limit? She doesn't hesitate before replying:

Oh, my! I can't ever imagine getting to the point of saying, "Gee, there's nothing more I can learn about this person, this country, this idea, this business of life." There are so many different viewpoints—like looking through a housefly's eye with all the multifaceted images, none of them exactly the same. Through each different prism the shift in view is ever so slight, ever so subtle, and ever so interesting.

I would tell host families that they need to be learners because there's always going to be something that trips them up, something that challenges them and challenges their view of themselves. Like me, they are going to stumble and fall and bang their shins. They need to expect to make mistakes, ask questions, ask for help, forgive themselves, and let themselves be challenged.

Endnotes

1. Personal communication in 1995 from Dr. F. Sushila Niles. At the time of her sojourn to Africa, Dr. Niles was teaching at an African university.

2. Described by Hall in *Beyond Culture,* 7. Westerners tend to rely on thought processes that consider only straight-line cause and effect relationships: "A" leads to "B." Exceptions, multiple correlations, and seemingly erratic or irrelevant information is generally ignored.

—17—

Stage Eight: Predeparture

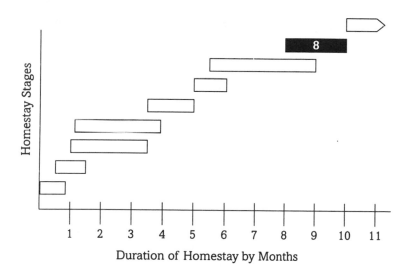

Duration of Homestay by Months

Stage Eight begins near the end of the homestay experience, approximately six weeks prior to the student's departure, and ends when the student leaves.

Sometimes families recoil at the very mention of the term *predeparture*. "The word has a stigma," says one host mother. "To most families, it's nothing more than just a nice word for the awfulness of goodbye."

Although sadness and tension should not be dismissed or minimized, our view of the predeparture stage is not, on the whole, negative. On the contrary, the final weeks are a time to put a good ending to an overall rewarding experience.

The ways that host families and students experience this stage vary dramatically. In many cases, a closeness develops, and special efforts are made to get the most out of the time remaining. In other cases, there is a loosening of bonds, resulting in a noticeable shift away from the comfortable relationships of previous months.

In the latter case, what often surfaces is discomfort, irritability, hypersensitivity, and defensiveness. "Your student begins to break all the rules, acting like a brat with a double-digit IQ," quips one host father. "Rightly or wrongly, you get the feeling of being ignored, as though you've been tossed out like yesterday's newspaper and your home is being used as a hotel."

Another host parent remarks,

> Things start to go to pot. Everyone starts bellyaching and nitpicking. One minute I'm dying to get the experience over and done with, so I try driving a mean wedge of anger between myself and our student. It's easy to do if I can convince myself I've been used and abused. "Good riddance," I broadcast to everyone.
>
> The next minute I'll be the complete opposite: possessive and jealous and ashamed about ever thinking of booting him out the door, coaxing him to stay forever and saying, "Everyone knows the stork made a mistake—he delivered you to the wrong place! You were always meant to be our kid."

About this same time, families receive official notification of the return flight schedule. "I glance at the letter but I don't pay any attention to it," reveals one mother who reacts to the news as an unwelcome aggravation.

> When the organization sends that letter, I think, "Why are they throwing cold water on our fantastic experience? Why did they send this information so early?"
>
> I worry that if I start thinking about the end I'll spend the last two months dragging around and feeling crummy. So I just stuff the letter in a clut-

tered drawer and tell myself that there'll be plenty
of time to deal with the end when the end is here.

Some families find that they can effectively push aside the
unpleasant news of their student's imminent departure and
continue coasting, but many families have learned that the
denial approach can create real heartaches, as another host
mother explains.

> Some families put off talking until their student's
> flight ticket arrives in July. That's a big mistake. By
> then the days have gotten too frantic and nerves
> too jangled to say the thoughtful things you really
> want to say.
>
> You'd think the last day would be the right time
> to say all the things you've been saving up for
> months, but it's not. The last day is pure madness,
> crammed with errands, friends popping in, and last-
> minute packing. Wearily you pile into the car and
> rush to the airport. "At last," you sigh, "there's time
> to talk." But there you are, standing in a crowded
> room of strangers, and you find you can't get the
> words out. So you stare at each other, awkwardly
> shake hands, and repeat worn, hollow phrases like
> "Have a safe trip."
>
> As the plane disappears, you console yourself
> with the thought, "I'll say everything in a letter."
> But you know you can't really. How can you punc-
> tuate a sentence with intimate eye contact or a ten-
> der hug?
>
> So the plane flies away, and you're left feeling
> strangely cheated. "Maria changed our lives so
> much," you whisper. "Why didn't I take the time to
> tell her?"

To avoid this heartache, it's a good idea to begin actively preparing for your student's departure. The task may be an unfamiliar one, so the following are some ways you can proceed.

Recognize Feelings

The goodbye process begins when the family starts seriously
examining their own thoughts and feelings about the impend-

ing departure. There may be a variety of reactions: irritation, relief, sadness, confusion, accomplishment, nervousness, or a jumbled mixture.

Accept Feelings of Loss

Frequently, family members find themselves vacillating between feelings of loss and gain. While they recognize that a solid friendship has been established (one that will endure despite separation), they also realize that when their student leaves, this experience of lifestyle sharing will end forever. Another host mother reflects on this bittersweet aspect.

> As the days evaporate, you're going to hurt, and you'll be convinced that you, not your student, are the one losing the most. Some days will be great, filled with celebration and tender remembrances; others will be just awful.
>
> You'll fret that once you've parted, the caring will stop, and you'll have a gnawing awareness that something will never be quite the same ever again. Through it all, you may be changed for the better: you may learn that it's okay to hurt deeply when you love.

Let Go

One host father likens saying goodbye to the experience of giving one's daughter away in marriage. In both cases, you're breaking one bond and sanctioning another. "It's not easy to do," the host father admits. "But for the marriage to work, the parent has to step down and assume a secondary role."

In much the same way, you'll need to relinquish your role as a host parent and return responsibility to your student's natural parents. This can be done by conveying to your student your recognition that she belongs with her natural family (even though in some ways, she may feel better understood by your family) and that she will soon again be involved in their lives. Through such messages, you will, in a very important way, be giving your student permission to return home.

Take Stock of the Homestay Experience

During your final weeks together, it's important to spend some time reviewing the year's experience. "We began scheduling informal evening talks," explains one host father, who said to his student, "Pier, we only have a few brief weeks left together, so let's talk about what it's been like—both the good and the bad moments. Let's explore what we've learned from the experience of living together."

As a part of this review, some families find it helpful to put together two identical scrapbooks of their shared experiences (one for the family to keep and one for the student to take with her). As photos and keepsakes are assembled, family members have a chance to share personal reactions, talk about what they've learned, and describe how they've changed. "It's really heartwarming to see tears in your student's eyes as she tells you this has been the best year of her life," reveals one host mother. Or, as another host mother reports, "All of a sudden I realized that our own daughter had gained two years' maturity during the six months our exchange student was with us. That felt good."

To top off the review, many families plan ways to celebrate their sense of accomplishment, success, and growth. Some arrange a special dinner; others give a party or share a quiet weekend together at a camp retreat.

Prepare Your Student for Reverse Culture Shock

It has been said that teenage exchange students travel to not one but two foreign cultures: the one they are visiting and the one they return to. What this means is the somewhat ironic notion that upon returning home, exchange students often find their own home culture strange and even forbidding.

As the departure date approaches, many students fluctuate between feeling quite jubilant and suffering pangs of apprehension. You can help by encouraging your student to discuss her concerns openly. One host mother explains to her students that it is normal for them to feel anxious about returning home. Then she helps them anticipate some of the issues they might face.

> You know your family will certainly notice that you've grown two inches taller, but they may not notice your growth in maturity. What will it be like for you if they don't recognize the inner changes and continue treating you exactly the same? If this becomes a problem for you, how can you help your parents begin to appreciate the ways you've changed? And if that doesn't work, what might you do next?

Other issues related to reverse culture shock that can be discussed include (1) the possibility of being criticized for appearing "Americanized," (2) feeling out of step with the changes that have taken place at home, (3) feeling awkward speaking one's native language again, (4) being ignored by old friends, (5) missing one's host family, (6) noticing the indifference most people at home will display toward one's international experience, (7) facing school exams, and (8) finding ways to integrate what has been learned into one's daily life.

While discussing these issues will not necessarily produce fail-safe solutions or totally immunize your student against reverse culture shock, it will hopefully reduce the number of unexpected jolts that are encountered. In addition, it may give her a feeling of confidence and optimism that she can deal with what lies ahead.

The Farewell

"Saying that final goodbye is never easy," explains a father who has hosted a dozen or more exchange students over the years. "No matter how thoroughly we review what's been gained, no matter how much we communicate to a student that the experience has been exceedingly special and rewarding, those last few hours are filled with intense emotion that words alone cannot adequately express."

To express symbolically what words alone cannot, some families give their student a farewell gift on the last day—

perhaps a locket, a hand-knit sweater, or a framed family photo. One family has developed the custom of giving their student a symbolic house key on which they inscribe a special message. Another family prepares a thoughtful letter and quietly slips it into their student's pocket before she boards the plane.

Sometimes students also say a special farewell by leaving behind a gift for the household or a hidden note to be discovered at some later date. One student left an expression of affection which she had penned on a sliver of cardboard and tacked to a closet door.

I'd like the memory
Of me
To be a happy one.
I'd like to leave
An afterglow
Of smiles.

When days are gone,
I'd like to leave
An echo
Whispering softly
Down the ways,
Of happy times
And laughing times.

I'd like the tears
Of those who grieve
To dry before the sun,
As happy memories
Linger on
When days are gone.

—18—

Stage Nine: Readjustment

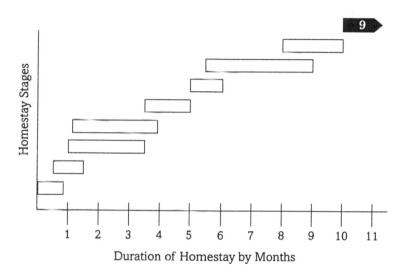

Duration of Homestay by Months

Stage Nine begins with the exchange student's departure and usually continues for three to six weeks. In some subtle ways, this stage
may continue for several months as the experience of hosting continues to influence the lives of family members.

"The hosting experience does not come to an end when you
say goodbye," states a seasoned host mother.

> You don't just drive home from the airport and re-
> sume your normal life. There are feelings to be ac-
> knowledged, new routines to be considered, and a
> relationship with your former exchange student
> which will need defining. All this takes time and
> work.

The ride home from the airport can itself be unsettling. Along with feelings of sadness, there's often a sensation of disbelief, an eerie numbness that gets expressed in the thought, "This isn't really happening, is it? Tomorrow our student will be back and everything will be fine again." One host father's description of the airport departure is typical.

> The ride home—it took forever. In the car, it was cold and quiet, like there had been a death in the family. Everybody was shaken by the emptiness, and everyone was crying a little bit. I didn't totally believe it, but I knew Heidi was gone. And I wondered if I would ever, ever see her again.

Families often experience a period of mourning, which may continue for several days or weeks. One person might appear sad and uncommunicative, while others might abound with nervous energy and worried thoughts like "Oh, I do hope Michio made her connecting flight in San Francisco" or "Sverrir must be back in Iceland now. I wonder if his girlfriend came to the airport to meet him. What if he's laughed at for speaking with an American accent?" One host father elaborates on the emotion-packed message he sent to his e-mail friends on an exchange student bulletin board.

> Our little Finnish Elf left Wednesday. We have hosted several students over the years, but for some reason, her departure has hit me particularly hard. My emotions are right at the surface, and when I remember special moments I feel either giddy or sad to the point of tears. There's an emptiness inside, knowing that someone special that I grew to admire so much is now absent from my life.
>
> And I worry about her—where she is and what she's doing. I'm no longer by her side to protect her, to support her, to encourage her. I feel like a father whose son or daughter has left for military duty, possibly dangerous duty. There's a terrible fear that I may never see her again.
>
> So here I am, a forty-six-year-old and experiencing homesickness without ever leaving home. Thank goodness we'll be visiting her this fall. I hope

> I can regain control of my emotions by then. (Much
> of this is written with tears rolling down my cheeks.)

A mother who has hosted fifteen students explains that the grieving process often centers around her former student's bedroom.

> For the first couple of weeks, I just avoided Jarl's
> bedroom. Only gradually did I feel strong enough
> to open the door and walk by. Then one day I went
> inside. I could hear his voice, and I just stood there
> and cried.

Another host mother states that she agonized for the first few weeks, having received no communication from her Middle Eastern student. "I became worried and anxious," she says, "thinking that maybe Hatam had fallen off the edge of the earth, or worse, maybe he had stopped caring for us." She describes her family's reactions.

> We had this intense longing because a part of our
> life was missing. Everywhere we looked we found
> emptiness—a bedroom was empty, a chair at the
> dinner table, a shelf in the bathroom cabinet. Ev-
> erywhere was the message: we've shrunk to one
> less.

A month after their student has left, most families find that they are beginning to return to normal. Generally, they are able to resume their routines, re-establish comfortable sched- ules, and interact as a family without intense feelings of loss. "You begin to realize that life will go on, and that you can enjoy being a smaller family again," notes one father.

Just when things start to settle down, however, the mail carrier may deliver the first letter from your former exchange student, throwing your family back into turmoil. One mother puts it this way:

> Every day we waited for the mail, so we were ec-
> static when an overseas letter finally arrived from
> Evy. But the message brought us down again, be-
> cause Evy wrote that she was lonely and unhappy
> and homesick for our family and life in the U.S.

With the hope of providing Evy with some soothing reassurance and insightful guidance, the mother began writing a lengthy response. But as she wrote page after page of advice, she began to realize the limitations of a letter. "It's not the same as a person-to-person dialogue," she explains. "And it hit me that by the time Evy got my response, she would probably have these problems solved and be dealing with new concerns."

Another mother experienced different frustrations with letter writing. She began mailing letters on a weekly basis but received only infrequent responses from her former exchange student. At first she felt annoyed and rejected by the student's "indifference" until she realized her motivations for writing were suspect. She was trying to sustain the relationship at a level which was no longer possible. She explains,

> I wrote Francisco every week because I wanted to keep him abreast of all the family's activities and experiences. I wanted to keep him involved in our lifestyle, but I think he was put off by my frenzied efforts. You see, I didn't want to accept the fact that we were no longer host parents sharing our home and way of life with him.

What both of these mothers came to realize through the experience of letter writing was the practical meaning of saying goodbye. Although each had seen her exchange student board the plane, neither had recognized the finality of that departure until she could no longer talk to her student about new ideas and feelings, offer timely advice, or share life experiences.

Eventually both mothers were able to accept the fact that the old way of relating no longer worked. In place of the hosting relationship, they began to enjoy a kind of pen-pal friendship, a friendship not unlike the lingering bond one often cherishes with an old college classmate or a childhood buddy. When this new arrangement was accepted, each family became comfortable with the idea of receiving one or two letters a year from their special overseas friend and perhaps an occasional e-mail message, or getting a phone call or photo as a Christmas treat.*

Just as parents often find that defining their relationship with a newly married son or daughter may take time, you might discover that it takes several months and deliberate effort to establish a sort of amiable but distant "absentee friendship" with your former exchange student. "It's not easy," acknowledges one host father, "but once you can let go of needing the relationship to continue, you can begin to savor the experience you had." He discovered that

> a part of Adriana left four years ago, but a part of her is ours and will be with us forever. She left a vast storehouse of memories that keep pouring out day after day, year after year. We find that we continue to use her quirky expressions, we remember events by things she did and said, and we see our mundane routines afresh through her innocence and intensity. Some things about the hosting experience have died, but not our memories. They are beautiful, alive, and very special.

Perhaps at Christmas several years from now, you will curl up in a chair and find just the right words to express your appreciation and love to that special young man or woman who once spent an eventful year in your home. And perhaps as you look back and remember, your sentiments will be similar to those of the host mother who wrote the following letter.

> December 21
>
> Dear Torben,
>
> How we wish you could be here next week to be the best man in Mark's wedding. We know that in your last year of medical school your life is extraordinarily busy. Nonetheless, as the wedding approaches, we feel your absence strongly. And we remember....

---

* It is also a sad fact that some students do not write after their return home.

We remember how you loved to swim, and how you always carried your bathing suit with you "just in case." We remember how you and Mark argued over who could consume the most ice cream. And who could forget the way you refused to go home? You just couldn't pack. Almost everything left the country bundled in your arms—coats, posters, clothes, souvenirs, you name it. And we remember when you brought your bride, Kirsten, for a visit. We were all ecstatic.

The memories: They go on and on....

We still miss you, even after seven years! We learned so much from having you. We learned about you and Denmark, of course. But we also learned so much about ourselves, our family and the United States. Best of all, we learned how people grow—and grow up. Some of that learning is still in progress for us. Maybe it will never end! Maybe growth is like the glistening beam of a flashlight that expands ever outward into the night.

Torben, we will miss you on the 27th, but in another way you will be with us, all day. We send you so much love, and our thanks for all you have given us. There is still a bond, and there always will be. Hurry back!

Much love,

Mary

Common Concerns

Money Issues

Exchange students from either affluent or economically struggling families may have difficulty adjusting to life in a middle-income American home. The affluent student might not realize that spending money at a breezy clip can create discomfort for her host family. As hosts, you may need to explain to her that carrying and spending a lot of money while living in your home will make her an outsider to your lifestyle and may alienate her from other teenagers in the community.

Conversely, the family may have difficulty being sensitive to the adjustment problems faced by a youngster who is used to a "privileged" life. If this becomes an issue, discuss the differences with the student. Try to develop an appreciation for her experience and ask her to try to accept any limitations that come from sharing your family's middle-class style of living.

Students from some cultures have scrimped and saved for the exchange program experience, and they may not have enough money to cover some of the special expenses that come up. Some exchange programs with active local volunteer organizations will help raise funds for students who might need help to purchase a senior ring, tickets to the prom, or even a winter coat.

Frequently students arrive with ample spending money but lack an understanding of how much their American dollars will buy, or they become overwhelmed by U.S. gadgetry and begin buying everything in sight. An unfortunate result is that some students run out of money by Christmas, just when they need to be buying winter clothes. One way to prevent this from happening is to help your student budget her money, but don't be too strict. Many students will want to buy gifts to take home. Money for such purchases shouldn't be included in a budget for routine expenses.

Who pays for what? Most programs require that students provide their own spending money. But for special trips and dining out, problems can arise because neither the student nor the family is quite sure who should pay.

With some advance planning this potentially thorny problem can be avoided. Discuss what you will be doing and how you want to share the expenses involved. Sometimes families are uncomfortable asking the student to pay when the whole family goes out for dinner, to the movies, or on weekend trips, so they end up doing fewer of these activities than they would like because of the costs involved. Other families feel very strongly that the student should contribute to the expenses incurred for these family outings. Often they ask the student to pay half or all of her own "special-occasion" expenses.

You may find it unpleasant to talk about such matters, but it seems there is no painless alternative. When a family is reluctant to pay but avoids talking about it, resentments and misunderstandings can, and often do, result.

Some host families give their exchange student an allowance, although many do not. What's important is that the exchange student have roughly the same amount of spending money as other teenagers in the family and/or the school community. If your student is from a wealthy family, they have probably given her more than enough money for her day-to-day expenses. Together, you can work out a weekly budget of typical expenses (movies, telephone, postage, toiletries) and help her stay within these guidelines.

Language Problems

Because many students have difficulty communicating in English, any help you can provide will probably be greatly appreciated. Even students who have studied English for many years make pronunciation mistakes or use American idioms and slang in inappropriate ways. For example, a Greek boy startled his host mother when he remarked, "We don't eat snakes in Greece like you do in the U.S." What brought about the mother's alarm was a mere language error—the boy had mispronounced the word *snacks*. Similarly, a Swedish girl gave her host family a chuckle when she explained, "In my country it's not customary to smell (smile) in pictures."

You also may have heard stories about the chagrined exchange student who referred to a pencil eraser as a "rubber," or of American teenage girls who, while trying to say that they had had enough to eat, instead accidentally announced to their French hosts that they were pregnant. On the surface, these are amusing anecdotes—as long as they happen to someone else. For the one who utters them, the experience can be humiliating.

You will no doubt wince at the thought of having to explain to your exchange student the difference between such words as clapped and crapped. But if you imagine yourself in the student's position, it will be easier for you to correct her in a comfortable manner.

If you just can't help laughing at the gaffe, start by apologizing, and then show your respect by recognizing her embarrassment and stating that you do understand the intent of her sentence. Last but not least, offer to explain the difference between the two apparently similar words. Another very effective strategy is to tell the student an amusing, embarrassing story about yourself. This bridges the awkwardness.

Other language errors may not seem amusing at all and may take longer to recognize for what they are. One host mother found herself stunned and even offended at the end of a complicated discussion of political philosophies. In a hushed tone, her Colombian exchange student leaned forward and remarked, "You are a very dense person." Fortunately, the mother's reaction was, he can't mean that! and after an awkward silence she asked, "What do you mean by *dense*? I don't think it has the same meaning for me as it does for you." As Francisco explained, she realized that he meant *deep*, not *dense*. No longer taken aback, she was then eager to explain the difference.

During your student's stay, don't be surprised if you're called upon repeatedly to define the meaning of unfamiliar words or to interpret popular expressions. Sojourners are often eager to learn the latest slang expressions and will try to use them, sometimes at their peril. After spending half the night trying out and giggling over "four-letter words," a host sister was left a bit wide-eyed and tense the next morning when her French counterpart casually threw one of the words into a family conversation. The French girl wasn't in "hot water" for long, but she did have some initial difficulty understanding why her American parents were so disgusted and embarrassed by a word which the French consider nothing but a mild curse.

There's not much you can do to prevent situations like these from occurring, but you *can* help your student develop greater fluency in English. Here are some suggestions: (1) encourage her to carry a small bilingual dictionary (or phrase book); (2) help her develop a curiosity for language by discussing the meaning of words and by helping her understand colorful expressions; (3) even though it may take your student a long time to compose her thoughts in English, be patient and try not to interrupt her, finish her sentences for her, or second-guess her answers; (4) speak simply (but not simplemindedly; your student is no doubt quite intelligent) and resist the temptation to solve communication problems by raising your voice—poor hearing is rarely the cause; (5) especially during the first weeks, try to avoid using idiomatic expressions, particularly those related to sports (such as *get to first base, go for the gold*, etc.); and (6) if your student's fluency is extremely low, ask the sponsoring organization if tutoring services are provided.

Re-placements to Second and Third Host Families

Although the majority of homestays are successful, there are cases in which the initial placement doesn't work out and the exchange student must be moved to one or more other host families. What little research there is indicates that roughly 30 percent of initial families will not keep their student for the entire experience.

While it may be unpleasant to think about losing a student, knowing that changes do occur with some frequency can help ease any possible feelings of failure.

When it becomes necessary for a student to move to a second host family, the transition can be eased if the reasons for leaving are openly discussed and blame is avoided. Everyone may feel relieved when the transition is completed, but it is important to bear in mind that saying goodbye may be difficult for everybody involved. Frequently, families as well as students feel sad, angry, guilty, and rejected for a period of time. After the student's departure, it is important for family members to evaluate the experience as a whole by identifying what was learned as well as what mistakes were made.

Some sponsoring organizations do not encourage families to contact students once they have moved. However, others do. In those cases, the friendship that has developed can continue.

Transportation

What American doesn't want wheels and the freedom they bring? If you live outside a major urban area, a car is essential. But foreign students may be prevented from driving by the exchange organization even if they have valid licenses from their home countries or take driver's education here. The result is that they are dependent on their host family and friends for most of their transportation needs. How do you handle it?

Often you will be able to provide a ride for your student. It is admittedly another adjustment to make in the family schedule, but you will find that time in the car can be a perfect opportunity to get to know this young person. Enjoy it!

To avoid feeling like a taxi service, rely occasionally on the classic carpool. Ask your student to make arrangements with other teenage drivers or the parents of younger teens. If there's uncertainty about which teen drivers to contact, ask your student's teachers to recommend a few responsible, reliable classmates. You can also enlist the help of relatives and friends. Yes, this will require extra effort on your part, but if you can help your student become acquainted with other people in the community, everyone will benefit from the experience.

If a public mode of transportation is available and practical, obtain schedules and fee information and take the time to help your exchange student understand how the system works.

What if you have the opposite situation? What if your exchange student is too shy to ask you to take her anywhere? One host family with a German boy discovered this problem. After much discussion, they convinced him that they expected to be asked to provide transportation and they would gladly offer or arrange for it.

Phone Calls

Being an exchange student often means the loss of some privileges. For example, most students are not allowed to drive a car in the United States, so they sometimes latch on to the telephone as a substitute way of socializing. Since phone calls can be expensive (especially when exchange students call other exchange students who live in other parts of the country), it's good to establish procedures regarding usage and payment.

Sometimes families worry that their exchange student will not make a good adjustment unless all phone contact with the natural parents is severed, and some sponsoring organizations stipulate that phone calls home are to be actively discouraged. Calls home, however, are important for most teenagers living away from their natural families. Still, students should not be encouraged to use calls home as a substitute for working out adjustment concerns. Good sense should be the guide here. Continued contact with natural families is conducive to a good adjustment. If phone calls home (or e-mail) increase in length and frequency, it may be a signal that problems have developed, in which case family discussions and/or counseling may be advised so that the student's adjustment can be eased.

Regarding procedures for handling the expense of phone calls, many families ask their students to use prepaid credit cards when making overseas and in-country long-distance calls or have their natural parents make the call.

It is also worth mentioning to your student the costs involved in some of the information and entertainment hot lines and other phone calls that a student may believe are "free" but which end up being very expensive. One host family ended up with over $200 of telephone calls when their exchange student called up several voice-mail boxes advertised in the personals column of the neighborhood newspaper. He had no idea that these calls cost money and was very embarrassed at the expense charged to his host family.

School Adjustment

Contending with school and the teenage subculture can be one of the biggest hurdles an exchange student encounters. She may have a difficult time understanding classroom lectures; be dazed by the frantic pace of students dashing madly from class to class every fifty minutes; feel threatened by the peer pressure to experiment with alcohol, sex, and drugs; and find the emphasis on extracurricular activities confusing.

It is often quite difficult for foreign students to understand what is considered appropriate classroom behavior. Many students come from cultures where the relationship with teachers is different, where competition and emphasis on individual effort is less evident, where little or no discussion occurs in the classroom, where definitions of cheating and plagiarism are different from our own, or where homework is nonexistent. In addition to these differences, even those who are nearly fluent in English find that it takes them substantially longer to complete their reading and writing assignments than it takes their American classmates. All of these factors can make it difficult for exchange students to achieve the level of academic performance they would back home. As hosts, you don't want to add to the pressure.

In addition, many schools will not give academic credit for overseas studies. For this reason, some exchange students have already completed their secondary schoolwork before their sojourn, and many others are simply losing a year in their academic program. It is sometimes difficult for these students to be motivated to complete their schoolwork here, and some are tempted to cut classes or complain about having to attend school. If you think your student is placed in classes that are not challenging enough, talk to the teachers and with representatives of the exchange organization.

American Parenting Styles

You will also want to be mindful of the fact that parenting styles vary from culture to culture, and your student may be puzzled, even shocked at times, by how you relate to your own children—seeing you as too lenient, too strict, or perhaps overprotective.

Compared to many Northern European cultures, U.S. parents tend to be fairly strict with their children. The parents provide most of the discipline, and teenagers are viewed as "large children," not as emerging adults. As the saying goes: under my roof, go by my rules. Because of these dynamics, it's argued that adolescence is not a time when American teenagers learn self-reliance. Some social psychologists believe that it is the intense fight for a modicum of independence that makes some American teenagers turn rebellious.

—B—

Bridging Skills

At times, conversations between people of different cultural backgrounds are punctuated with discord and misunderstanding. But it doesn't have to be this way. With the use of bridging skills, individuals can communicate effectively—despite the lack of a shared cultural heritage.

To develop this special fluency is not easy and often requires training, which we hope will become more and more accessible through the organizations that sponsor student exchanges. Bridging skills can enhance your ability to show respect and tolerance for differences. For a successful hosting experience, there is nothing more important than a strong repertoire of these skills.

If you have not had the opportunity to learn about these skills in a training course, we offer a list of the most important ones. One of the skills, "Watch for red alerts," was presented in chapter 6. Two others—"Don't apply the Insult Rule" and "Don't trivialize trivial misunderstandings"—were described in chapter 12. Nine more follow.

Use Empathy

Empathy—a skill we all have but don't use enough—is the ability to step outside of our own experience and into the experience of someone else. It requires that we temporarily put aside our own feelings, opinions, or perspective and deliberately try to see things from a different point of view.

Empathy also requires careful listening and attentiveness, because we must gather information from the other person before we can truly understand his or her experience.

One of the most important ways to express empathy is to paraphrase or restate what you have heard. Another way is to identify the other person's feelings and acknowledge them, thereby conveying that you understand and respect the other's experience.

"It was a look in Marja's eyes and her slight hesitation." That's what prompted one host father to reach out—in an empathetic way—to his exchange student when she was unsure about what to say when she called to sign up for a driver's education class. He elaborates.

> Being Finnish, the quality of *sisu*[*] was very important to Marja, so she was determined to face her fear and to conquer it. Still, I could tell that she was uncertain and nervous about what she had to do. Seeing this in her, I suggested that we rehearse it. So we role-played the phone call that she needed to make. Then I stood by with moral support when she made the actual call.

Remember, empathy is a skill. The more you practice using it, the more natural it will become and the easier it will be to relate in this special way.[†] Without empathy, we can be emotionally tone-deaf to many of the subtle social signals of others.

Learn to Shift Your Perspective

In a moment, we want you to look at some words which probably will not appear readable as an intelligible sentence, chiefly

---

[*] *Sisu* is a prized character trait of the Finns, expressed as a stoic determination to face challenges with an inner strength.

[†] A word of caution. Discussing feelings doesn't always work. Sometimes cultures—including that of the United States—teach people that to show certain emotions or talk about feelings is a sign of weakness. Be alert to these differences. If you sense discomfort, check out your perception and, if necessary, shift your focus to a discussion of behavior, which is often less threatening and more acceptable.

because of the intrusion of apparently meaningless black marks that either distract, confuse, or intrigue you. But this *is* a legitimate sentence. Look at it carefully to see if you can figure out the meaning (before we solve the mystery in the next paragraph).

That hot-fudge sundae has a ı ⊐ ▶⁺◀ on it.

In order to read the mystery word, you have to make a mental and visual shift in perspective—from reading black letters on a white background (the usual format) to reading white letters on a black background. The shift we are talking about must occur in order to read the word *fly.*

Cultural differences are like the word *fly* in that they defy conventional perception. So in order to understand some aspect of your student's behavior, you may need to take an imaginative leap into a different point of view. The use of contexting questions, which are described next, can help you "get off the ground."

Use Contexting Questions

As we have mentioned previously, it is easy to misinterpret meaning and arrive at the wrong conclusions, and it is especially easy to do so when engaged in cross-cultural communication. To minimize this problem, ask for clarification—about words, assumptions, and cultural patterns. Try to get in the habit of saying, "Perhaps I don't understand this from your perspective. Can you tell me more about what you mean?"

Be Open-Minded

Having an exchange student in your home means being exposed to new ideas and new information, which can be approached with open-mindedness or closed-mindedness. If we tend to automatically shut out new information, we are using a thought pattern that reflects closed-mindedness. Intercultural specialists say that culture itself tends to produce closed-mindedness. The result? New information and differences of opinion are labeled as deviations from what is "normal" or "right." To become open-minded requires practice and a con-scientious effort to overcome culture's conditioning.[1]

"Elisabeth came to us with 'wild blue yonder' ideas," ex-plains one host mother as she describes her struggle to be open-minded with her German student's "idealistic" views.

> Elisabeth professed that the perfect society was hunter-gatherers, that back-to-nature was the pana-cea for civilization's ills. At first I found this very irritating because what she said seemed so off base. It seemed to make no sense at all to me, and it took me a long time to get past my frustration.
>
> But I listened and I learned that Elisabeth was trying out new ideas. I realized that eventually she would consider many alternatives before deciding which ideas had real merit and which didn't. But first she needed to have the freedom to explore, to deviate from conventional, straight-ahead thinking.
>
> We all need that freedom, and I'm told it's something that German schools in particular are promoting. Teachers want to make sure their young people will never march in lockstep ever again.

Don't Store Up Grievances

> An Indonesian middle-class boy fell in love with an upper-class girl, and they wanted to marry. One day the boy's mother went to the house of the girl's mother for tea. A banana was served with the tea, which was a most unusual combination. The women did not discuss the wedding plans during their visit, but the boy's mother knew that it was off: bananas do not go with tea.[2]

It might seem that the girl's mother went to great lengths just to get her point across. But all cultures—including that of the United States—have social taboos against discussing unpleas-ant topics, especially with people we don't know very well. As a rule, we are taught "Just keep quiet and get along." That's why it can be so difficult to mention things to your student when he does or says something that annoys you. In these situations, hosts will often try to give subtle hints or will simply overlook and dismiss matters of disagreement. But in a family living situation like hosting, this approach seldom works for long. And it often leads to bigger problems, as one host father explains.

> It is unpleasant to sit down and talk about a problem. Hence we tend to let them pile up. Then, when we can't take any more and one glaring incident occurs, we go over the anger edge. We just explode.
> Problems should not be catalogued. Problems are best handled and disposed of as they occur and should not be ignored or filed away. Doing so makes them very dangerous.

To keep your relationship with your student on safe ground, you will want to make a commitment to yourself to address problems early. Talk them out, reach an understanding, and make sure that all parties follow through on agreed-upon changes. Try to do this every time something upsets you.[‡]

Here's something more to consider: each time you work out a disagreement, you will be accomplishing more than you may think; you will also be crossing what we call "deepening points" in the relationship, taking the relationship to a deeper level of trust, rapport, and commitment. You see, by talking things out, you are conveying an unspoken message: "You are important to me and so is your friendship. I don't want any hard feelings to come between us." And the result? It will probably get easier to talk about disagreements the next time around.

Use Open-Ended Questions

When seeking information, there are two different kinds of questions you can use: closed-ended (e.g., "Do you have cars in your country?") or open-ended ("What kinds of transportation are common in your country?") By using the former,

---

[‡] If you or your student find that routine problem solving is too much to handle, it is a likely warning signal that the hosting relationship is in jeopardy. Such a statement may sound quite strong, but we believe that this bridging skill is crucial.

you will get yes or no answers, you will be discouraging back-and-forth dialogue, and your questions can easily be misconstrued as being offensive (because your student may conclude there are simplistic assumptions behind them).

This happened to Henríque, a Brazilian student, who was repeatedly asked by his classmates, "Does your father grow coffee beans in the jungle?" In some cases, the question may have been intended as a veiled insult. In other instances, it was probably asked out of naiveté and genuine curiosity. But for the young Brazilian, the question was "stupid." Closed-ended questions tend to be taken just that way. As much as possible, try to keep your questions open-ended (by starting your inquiries with the words *what, when, how, why,* or *where*),[§] and try to teach this skill to your own children. This way you may get broader information and also avoid foot-in-mouth disease, which can be so distasteful.

Avoid the Rush to Judgment

To most Americans, being self-confident typically means being deliberate and decisive, forging ahead at full speed. But in cross-cultural interactions, a more tentative, cautious approach is often best. Because of the complexity of communication, the effect of culturally different thought processes, and the ever-present impact of cultural rules, scripts, and assumptions, try to slow things down a bit and keep an eye out for potential interference. As our legal system admonishes, avoid the rush to judgment.

So if you sense some contradiction or something puzzling going on, try not to make snap judgments. The operative words here are *hold your horses. Don't trample on the facts.* As an example, a lot of heartache could have been prevented for a Mexican boy, Carlos, and his host family had they heeded this advice. When it was discovered that Carlos had three brothers and two sisters and not five brothers as he had written on his application, he was accused of lying. His host family—

[§] These are known as "*wh* questions" because so many of them begin with the letters *wh.*

who had accumulated a gunnysack of minor complaints—used his "lying" to report him to the sponsoring organization.

But Carlos wasn't lying. While filling out the application in English, he had used Spanish logic, where the word *hermanos* can mean either "brothers" or "siblings." In English, he presumed that he was saying "I have five siblings."[||] Had this information been uncovered by his hosts or the support personnel, they could have understood Carlos's behavior and quite possibly prevented the damage caused by a rush to judgment.

It is easy to say things like "Consuela did that because she is lazy" or "This proves that Carlos was lying" or "What do you expect from Henryk? He's just inconsiderate." But such conclusions are usually wrong. They are character-trait judgments, called "blaming the person, ignoring the facts." They rely on short-circuited logic and can kick in almost automatically when we want quick answers and easy explanations.[#] Of course, the alternative can be cumbersome and tedious; we all know that it is much harder to deal with the entangling complexity of human experience when a true search for the facts is undertaken.

Learn to Ring Bells

When something that is said or done makes sense to us, it's because the event reminds us of something we already know. It rings our inner bell of past experience. So to understand your student's cultural patterns, it helps if you can identify a parallel pattern that we use in the United States for similar

---

[||] There are parallels in English. The English word *men* also has two meanings, depending on the context. For example, when Americans say "All men are created equal," they are using a masculine noun (men) to describe people (both men and women). This usage, although common, is not approved by all. Many women insist that it is tacitly discriminatory.

[#] The term for this kind of mistake is *attribution error*, attributing the wrong motive or cause to a behavior or situation. It has been popularized by Lee Ross, professor of psychology and an associate with the Stanford Center on Conflict and Negotiation.

situations. By doing so, those "strange foreign ways" will begin to ring a bell of familiarity. What's more, when you can find cultural parallels and share them, everyone starts to feel closer. As one host father puts it, "This sharing often results in a good laugh for all, as well as deeper understanding."

Incidentally, you may have noticed that this strategy is used throughout the book when presenting various cross-cultural examples, as with Carlos on the previous page. We included the footnoted explanation of the word *men,* hoping to tap into your own experience. Once you see the parallel in English, you then can say to yourself, "That boy's experience makes sense to me. It rings a bell."

Build a Repertoire of Understood Behaviors

The more you can use the bridging skills and attitudes that we have presented, the more fluent you will become in communicating across cultures. In the process you'll develop a rudimentary understanding of your student's cultural rules. And when this happens, your student's behavior will begin to seem more "logical." What's more, you'll find shorthand ways to alert each other to cultural differences when they arise. Gradually you will be in sync more and more of the time. And that will feel good to both of you.

Endnotes

[1] Terry Morrison, Wayne A. Conaway, and George A. Borden, *Kiss, Bow, or Shake Hands* (Holbrook, MA: Adams Media, 1994), xi-xii.

[2] Harlan Cleveland, G. J. Mangone, and J. G. Adams, *The Overseas Americans* (New York: McGraw-Hill, 1960), 79.

—C—

RADAR to the Rescue

RADAR* is the name of a strategy that can be used to help identify cross-cultural misunderstandings between host families and their students. To use the strategy, read through the five steps described below. The steps are followed by a real-life example of how RADAR helps with problem resolution.

> R=Red Alert
> A=Attitude Adjustment
> D=Discerning Detective
> A=About-Face
> R=Rules: Ours and Theirs

R=Red Alert

When nerves get frayed and your student starts to get under your skin, chances are a red alert is being sounded—either by you, your spouse, your student, or one of your children. A red alert is like a red flag; it serves as a warning.

Remember that red alert signals are often expressed as emotional reactions. As you think about the problem, try to

---

* This technique has been developed by the authors. It is based on their cross-cultural counseling expertise, numerous intercultural bridging concepts, and on a strategy developed by Elijah Lovejoy, retired from the University of California at Santa Barbara. See Cornelius Grove, *Orientation Handbook for Youth Exchange Programs* (Yarmouth, ME: Intercultural Press, 1989), 149-56.

identify your emotions. Are you feeling rejected, angry, insulted, confused, or just generally upset?

Once you have identified the emotion and formulated some opinions and maybe even some conclusions about the nature of the misunderstanding, move on to the next step of the RADAR strategy.

A=Attitude Adjustment

It's time to make an attitude adjustment. You know how complex everyday communication is and how easily our deeply embedded cultural patterns can cause interference. Stop and ask yourself these important questions:

- Could my conclusions/impressions about my student's behavior be wrong?

- Am I expecting my student to follow a rule that she might not know about (or has forgotten)?

- Do I sincerely want to try to work this out?

You'll become more neutral by (1) adopting a cautious attitude and by (2) accepting that maybe you are expecting your student to behave like a "good American." You also need an open-minded attitude and the ability to admit you aren't always right. Before moving on, ask yourself, "Could I possibly be wrong?"

D=Discerning Detective

The facts: that's what you're after at this stage. You want to start an objective investigation. At the first stage of this process, you started with some impressions and conclusions. Now you must get to the facts, which are the observable events, the descriptions of actual behavior. Leave behind your red alert reactions and become an impartial observer, focusing solely on what actually occurred. Like a detective, return to the scene and jot down your observations. Be as objective as possible. Don't rush past this step. This is where you attempt to step back from earlier emotion-based judgments and try to make sense of the information you have. This is not an easy step, but it's very important.

A=About-Face

During the About-Face stage, your empathy skills will come in handy. Ask your student for her side of the story, for her experience. Point out that you are trying to be neutral, to gather information. You don't want to give the impression that your intent is to get enough information so you can then accuse her of some wrongdoing. If that message is conveyed, you'll get back nothing but defensiveness.

R=Rules: Ours and Theirs

In this fifth step, attention shifts to our inner cultural guidebooks and their rules. Identify the American cultural norms that apply and ask your student to try to identify her cultural norms. As you discuss things, first explain the American rules that would apply to your particular situation, then ask questions that help your student identify her cultural patterns— the rules, values, and assumptions that will help explain her behavior; for example, you might say, "I need to understand. What's the rule for how this kind of situation is handled in your country?"

Once you have a good understanding of the rule, ask your student to verify that it is correct. Once cultural differences have been identified, it becomes possible to work out new agreements. In some instances, modifications on both sides may be in order. The end goal is to restore communication and goodwill. The following is a real-life example of how the RADAR approach may be used.

Putting RADAR to Work

As cross-cultural counselors, we were frequently contacted when a hosting relationship was in serious need of repair. In one fairly typical case, we were told something like the following: "Celso has become impossible. He's an obnoxious pest and obviously lonely. He's definitely immature—not exchange student material."

The use of such emotionally loaded red alert words as *obnoxious pest* and *immature* was a tip-off that the host family had reached the danger point. Our first task was to identify and acknowledge the intensity of everyone's emotions. To ignore someone's feelings is like erasing a good part of their experience. What's more, it's difficult to move to the next stage as long as intense feelings cloud perceptions and short-circuit thinking. Acknowledging feelings and identifying the family's impressions are part of the Red Alert step in RADAR.

Initially, we met with the student and family separately, giving each side a chance to speak freely. After each side had had an opportunity to air its grievances, each began to cool off, allowing the parties to move to the Attitude Adjustment stage. Both the host family members and the student acknowledged that they might have made mistakes, and each indicated a strong interest in working things out.

Next came the Discerning Detective step in which we asked the host parents what Celso was doing that gave the family the impression he was an "obnoxious pest." This took considerable detective work, but eventually they said, "He pesters his host sister when she is out with her friends." Their use of the negative word *pester* was a red alert reaction. Eventually, with additional detective work, this factual description emerged: "He doesn't have his own friends, so he hangs around with his host sister and her friends, and he lets her know if she does things he doesn't approve of."

Now the description was objective, and the parents and student were ready for the About-Face step—that is, it was time to get Celso's perspective. Here is what the parents discovered: Celso didn't think he was pestering his sister at all! Instead, he explained, "Where I live in Brazil, brothers and sisters and their friends all go out together. If my sister does something wrong, I should say something to her."

With the two descriptions of behavior in hand, we proceeded to the last step, Rules: Ours and Theirs. You will have no trouble recognizing the American rule.

> U.S. teenagers demonstrate their maturity by becoming independent, especially in their relationships with their parents and siblings. Consequently, a brother shouldn't interfere with his sister's activi-

ties. And a brother shouldn't discipline; that's the parents' job.

And the rule in Brazil?

Brazilian teenagers show maturity by demonstrating how well they can get along in a group of their siblings and extended family members. Consequently, teenagers and their close friends socialize together in groups, and the group itself is expected to keep its members in line. If a sister misbehaves, her brother is expected to say something to her; this is his responsibility. She will do the same. Only very serious infractions are reported to parents.

By Brazilian standards, Celso was being a good brother, but he made the mistake of using his Brazilian customs with his American host sister, who did not understand or like this pattern of behavior. Once identified, it became obvious that each culture had its own definitions of "responsible" ways for siblings to interact. Discussing these differences with Celso and his hosts brought about an end to their impasse and started the process of restoring their relationship.

By learning to use RADAR and teaching this strategy to your student, you will gain a valuable skill. Having a definable process to follow when problems arise will enhance your sense of confidence and help eliminate needless confusion.

—D—

Thinking of Hosting
an Exchange Student?

If you are interested in hosting an exchange student but have not made a final decision, you may want to know what you can do to improve your family's chances of becoming involved with a responsible, quality program. To help you make that choice, some suggestions are listed below.

1. *Meet with School Officials.* Contact your high school principal or school counselor to get a profile of the organization and to find out whether or not the school accepts students affiliated with the organization.

2. *Talk with Experienced Families.* Ask experienced host families if the program's support services were adequate and if promised services were available and helpful.

3. *Learn about Policies.* Ask the organization to provide information on the following: the criteria used to select students; the timing of host family placements (should be completed prior to the student's arrival in the United States); the schedule of orientation and predeparture sessions; and the kind of routine contact the organization maintains with the student and host family.

4. *Ask about Special Services.* Find out what special services the organization provides to students and families when problems and emergencies arise. Inquire about the following: Is medical insurance provided by the program?

Are counseling services available? Is there a hot-line number to call? Does the organization maintain a special financial account for emergencies? If so, does the account guarantee travel home if an emergency early return is required? If the student arrives with minimal English, are language classes or tutors provided?

5. *Meet with Your Local Representative.* Since a local representative will be your link to the sponsoring organization and its support services, it is important that the local representative live in your community and be trained to help with normal adjustment concerns. This person should also be someone with whom you feel comfortable. Remember that the representative's objectivity is crucial: if a friend or neighbor who is a representative should ask you to take a student, you might agree but ask that a different representative be assigned to help you and your student.

6. *Identify the Mission of the Program.* Programs that promote travel and adventure as their primary goal may not provide needed orientation or support services.

7. *Evaluate the Promotional Materials.* Beware of programs that emphasize fun and adventure without presenting a realistic picture of both stresses and rewards. If the literature erroneously describes its United States Information Agency (USIA) designation status by referring to it as a special endorsement or "U.S.-approved program," remember that a designation number from USIA is not a stamp of approval and to imply otherwise is misleading.

8. *Learn How Students Are Assigned.* Determine what steps will be taken to achieve a good match between your family and the student you host. Ask to receive background data and arrival information on the student at least three weeks prior to the date of the student's arrival in the United States so that you will have time to make contact and begin the "getting acquainted" process that gets the new relationship off to a good start.

9. *Inquire about Special Services for Hosts.* Reputable exchange organizations usually offer orientation opportunities and literature to prepare the family and provide practical guidance. Special counseling and support services should be available for families who host *at-risk* students.

10. *Ask for the USIA Regulations.* According to the USIA guidelines, host families must be provided with a copy of the current federal regulations (see page 185 for the address).

11. *Ask for Important Statistics.* You may want to request the following statistics: (1) the number of students assigned to your local area representative (when large numbers are assigned, it can be difficult for the representative to take a personal interest in the student or your family's needs), (2) the percentage of students who arrive without preassigned permanent families, (3) the percentage of re-placements to second and third families, (4) the percentage of students who require counseling, and (5) the early-return rates.

12. *Check Financial Records.* Many of the organizations state that their financial records are available for audit by responsible parties. If so, you might want to inquire about how the program fee is spent and what the salary range is for executive employees.

13. *Evaluate Each Program on Its Own Merits.* Don't automatically assume that proprietary programs are exploitative or that nonprofit programs are responsibly run. There are quality programs in both categories.

14. *Inquire about the Costs to the Student.* Because baseline program fees vary, you should check with individual organizations for prices. Bear in mind that in addition to the program fee, student costs include the money they are expected to bring for personal expenses: roughly 80 percent of the program fee for students on ten-month homestays; approximately 60 percent of the

program fee for those participating in shorter visits (six weeks to six months).

15. *Inquire about the Costs to the Host Family.* Although European programs frequently pay host families, U.S. programs rarely do. If the promotional materials claim that you need only provide room, board, and love, ask how much this may amount to financially. Many families report that the cost of hosting a student for the typical ten-month homestay is approximately 80 percent of the student's program fee. This amount excludes special trips or expensive gifts. For shorter homestays, the cost would be approximately 60 percent of the program fee.

16. *Clarify Your Reasons for Getting Involved.* When a family takes an exchange student for the wrong reasons or has unrealistic expectations about what the homestay experience will be like, disappointment and failure can result. Discuss your motivations openly and talk to experienced host families to learn if your plans seem realistic. (Expectations are described in chapter 11.)

17. *Consider Your Family's Current Situation.* While hosting a foreign student can be a rewarding, enjoyable experience, bear in mind that hosting is also expensive and stressful. If you are planning a move, if there is illness in the family, if a spouse is unemployed, or if your marriage is a bit shaky, now may not be the best time to invite an exchange student into your home. Carefully evaluate your family's readiness for the hosting experience so that you maximize the potential for its success.

18. *Give Thought to the Decision.* After you are interviewed by the sponsoring organization, postpone making a final decision until you have all the information you feel you need and until you have had adequate time to consider the decision thoroughly.

19. *Avoid Being Pressured.* Sometimes families feel emotionally coerced into a premature decision because they

are told a student is here and waiting for a home. Concern for a "homeless" exchange student is commendable, but it is not a sufficient reason to enter into a homestay experience. Try to base your decision on healthy motivations that take into consideration what's best for your family.

20. *Insist on Complete Information.* It is important that you have a thorough understanding of what your responsibilities and those of the sponsoring organization will be. As you are probably aware, this is known as informed consent; we think you should have it. Some organizations will ask you to sign a document confirming that you have been provided with complete information.

Agencies Providing Information on Exchange Programs

To research the quality of a particular program or to obtain information about the kinds of complaints, if any, that have been lodged against it, contact one of the following:

United States Information Agency (USIA)
Office of the General Counsel
The Exchange Visitor Program Office
Program Designation Branch
301 4th Street SW, Room 734
Washington, DC 20547
Phone: (202) 401-9810
Internet web page: http://www.usia.gov

Request the continually updated "Organizations with High School Exchange Visitor Program Designation" list and a copy of the federal regulations for student foreign exchange programs. The agency assigns designation numbers to programs meeting its minimum requirements. However, a USIA designation should not be considered a recommendation.

The National Association of Secondary School
Principals (NASSP)
Partners International Division
1904 Association Drive
Reston, VA 22091
Phone: (703) 860-0200

NAASP offers program evaluations through its Partners International division. Students and host families may speak to program managers for specific
countries. U.S. program managers handle inquiries
about exchanges to the United States.

Council on Standards for International Educational
Travel (CSIET)
212 South Henry Street
Alexandria, VA 22314
Phone: (703) 739-9050
Fax: (703) 739-9035

CSIET lists its U.S.-based member organizations
that provide teenage exchange programs. It as-
sesses the quality of these programs and publishes
annually the *Advisory List of International Educational Travel and Exchange Programs*. The council
can provide you with its list of standards for acceptable exchange programs at a small cost.

—E—

Suggested Reading List

Adler, Peter. "Beyond Cultural Identity: Reflections upon Cultural and Multicultural Man." In *Culture Learning: Concepts, Applications, and Research*, edited by Richard W. Brislin. Honolulu: University Press of Hawaii, 1977.

Aldrich, Robert A., and Glenn Austin. *Grandparenting for the 90s*. Escondido, CA: Robert Erdmann, 1991.

Althen, Gary. *American Ways*. Yarmouth, ME: Intercultural Press, 1988.

Austin, Clyde, ed. *Cross-Cultural Reentry: A Book of Readings*. Abilene, TX: Abilene Christian University, 1986.

Barna, LaRay M. "Stumbling Blocks to Intercultural Communication." In *Intercultural Communication: A Reader*, 5th ed., edited by Larry Samovar and Richard E. Porter, 322-30. Belmont, CA: Wadsworth, 1988.

Bellah, Richard, et al. *Habits of the Heart: Individualism and Commitment in American Life*. Berkeley: University of California Press, 1985.

Bennett, Janet M. "Transition Shock: Putting Culture Shock in Perspective." *International and Intercultural Communication Annual 4* (1977): 45-52.

Bennett, Milton J. "Overcoming the Golden Rule: Sympathy and Empathy." In *Communication Yearbook 3*, edited by D. Nimmo, 407-22. Philadelphia: International Communication Association, 1979.

─────. "Towards Ethnorelativism: A Developmental Model of Intercultural Sensitivity." In *Education for the Intercultural Experience*, 2d ed. edited by R. Michael Paige, 21-71. Yarmouth, ME: Intercultural Press, 1993.

Brislin, Richard W. *Cross-Cultural Encounters: Face-to-Face Interaction*. New York: Pergamon Press, 1981.

─────. "The Benefits of Close Intercultural Relationships." In *Human Assessment and Cultural Factors*, edited by S. H. Irvine and John W. Berry. New York: Plenum Publishing, 1983.

Brislin, Richard W., and H. Van Buren. "Can They Go Home Again?" In *Cross-Cultural Reentry: A Book of Readings*, edited by Clyde Austin, 219-29. Abilene, TX: Abilene Christian University, 1986.

Carroll, Raymond. *Cultural Misunderstandings: The French-American Experience*. Chicago: University of Chicago Press, 1988.

Cleveland, Harlan, G. J. Mangone, and J. G. Adams. *The Overseas Americans*. New York: McGraw-Hill, 1960.

Condon, John, and Fathi Yousef. *An Introduction to Intercultural Communication*. New York: Bobbs-Merrill, 1975. (out of print)

Fersh, Seymour. *Learning about Peoples and Cultures*. Evanston, IL: McDougal & Littell, 1974. (out of print)

Fieg, John P., and John G. Blair. *There Is a Difference: 17 Intercultural Perspectives*. Washington, DC: Meridian House International, 1980. (out of print)

Furnham, Adrian. "The Adjustment of Sojourners." In *Cross-Cultural Adaptation: Current Approaches*, edited by Young Y. Kim. Newbury Park, CA: Sage, 1988.

Gardner, G. H. "Cross-Cultural Communication." *Journal of Social Psychology* 58, (1962): 241-56.

Garza-Guerrero, A. C. "Culture Shock: Its Mourning and the Vicissitudes of Identity." *Journal of the American Psychoanalytic Association* 22, no. 2 (1974): 422-23.

Goodwin, Craufurd D., and Michael Nacht. "Fondness and Frustration: The Impact of American Higher Education on Foreign Students with Special Reference to the Case of Brazil." ITE Research Report Series No. 5. Ann Arbor: Books on Demand, 1986.

Gorden, Raymond. *Living in Latin America*. Skokie, IL: National Textbook, 1974.

Grove, Cornelius. *Orientation Handbook for Youth Exchange Programs*. Yarmouth, ME: Intercultural Press, 1989.

Hall, Edward T. *The Silent Language*. New York: Anchor/Doubleday, 1959.

————. *The Hidden Dimension*. New York: Anchor/Doubleday, 1966.

————. *Beyond Culture*. New York: Anchor/Doubleday, 1976.

Hood, Mary Ann G., Kevin Schieffer, and Martin Limbird. *Professional Integration: A Guide for Students from the Developing World*. Washington: NAFSA Association of International Educators, 1993.

Howard, Jane. *Families*. New York: Simon and Schuster, 1978.

Kauffman, Norman, Judith N. Martin, and Henry D. Weaver with Judy Weaver. *Students Abroad: Strangers at Home: Education for a Global Society*. Yarmouth, ME: Intercultural Press, 1992.

Klineberg, Otto, and W. Frank Hull IV. *At a Foreign University—An International Study of Adaptation and Coping*. Westport: Greenwood Publishing, 1979.

Kluckhohn, Florence R., and Fred L. Strodtbeck. *Variations in Value Orientation*. New York: Row, Petersen, 1961.

Kohls, L. Robert. *Survival Kit for Overseas Living*. 3d ed. Yarmouth, ME: Intercultural Press, 1996.

Lambert, Richard. *Educational Exchange and Global Competence*. New York: CIEE, 1994.

Lanier, Alison. Revised by Charles W. Gay. *Living in the USA*. 5th ed. Yarmouth, ME: Intercultural Press, 1996.

Lewis, Tom, and Robert Jungman, eds. *On Being Foreign*. Yarmouth, ME: Intercultural Press, 1986.

Marshall, Terry. *The Whole World Guide to Language Learning*. Yarmouth, ME: Intercultural Press, 1989.

Miller, Brent, and David Olson. *Family Studies: Review Yearbook*. Beverly Hills, CA: Sage, 1983.

Morrison, Terry, Wayne A. Conaway, and George A. Borden. *Kiss, Bow, or Shake Hands*. Holbrook, MA: Adams Media, 1994.

Olson, David H., and Hamilton I. McCubbin & Associates. *Families: What Makes Them Work*. Newbury Park, CA: Sage, 1989.

Paige, R. Michael, ed. *Education for the Intercultural Experience*. 2d ed. Yarmouth, ME: Intercultural Press, 1994.

Platt, Polly. *French or Foe? Getting the Most out of Visiting, Living and Working in France*. Culture Crossings, 1995.

Putnam, Robert D. "Bowling Alone: America's Declining Social Capital." *Journal of Democracy* 6, no. 1 (1995): 65-78.

Rhinesmith, Stephen H. *Bring Home the World: A Management Guide for Community Leaders of International Exchange Programs*. New York: Walker, 1986.

Rubin, Joan, and Irene Thompson. *How to Be a More Successful Language Learner*. Boston: Heinle & Heinle, 1982.

Samovar, Larry, and Richard E. Porter, eds. *Intercultural Communication: A Reader*. 8th ed. Belmont, CA: Wadsworth, 1997.

Singer, Marshall. "Culture: A Perceptual Approach." In *Intercultural Communication: A Reader*, 4th ed., edited by Larry Samovar and Richard E. Porter. Belmont, CA: Wadsworth, 1985.

Smith, Elise, and Louise Fiber Luce, eds. *Toward Internationalism*. 2d ed. Cambridge, MA: Newbury House, 1987.

Stewart, Edward C., and Milton J. Bennett. *American Cultural Patterns: A Cross-cultural Perspective*. Rev. ed. Yarmouth, ME: Intercultural Press, 1991.

Storti, Craig. *The Art of Crossing Cultures*. Yarmouth, ME: Intercultural Press, 1990.

———. *The Art of Coming Home*. Yarmouth, ME: Intercultural Press, 1997.

Weaver, Gary. *Culture, Communication and Conflict.* 2nd ed. New York: Simon and Schuster, 1997.

Zongren, Liu. *Two Years in the Melting Pot.* San Francisco: China Books and Periodicals, 1984.

Index

About the Authors

Nancy King and Ken Huff aren't newcomers to the fields of intercultural training and international youth exchange. This husband and wife worked together as cross-cultural counselors for a major youth exchange organization, conducting intercultural training seminars for employees, meeting with students and families to resolve cultural misunderstandings, and speaking at host family orientation sessions.

Nancy's intercultural case-study research took her to South America, and both Nancy and Ken earned doctorates from Wayne State University in counseling. For many years they were in private practice as mental health counselors and consultants in empathy and communication skills training, as well as corporate quality-of-work-life training programs.

Their backgrounds in journalism include freelance writing for the *Detroit News* and various magazines including *Time, Discover, People,* and *Fortune.* Currently Nancy writes feature stories for a national magazine targeted to the seniors' market.

For the past 15 years they have lived in central Florida, where they are in close contact with many host families and former exchange students. They would enjoy receiving your hosting comments and experiences. You may e-mail them at NBKing@AOL.com.